To Scott

Thanks for the
Support, holmes !

J-Zone

2012
RFTV

Root For the VILLAIN
RAP, BULLSHIT, AND A CELEBRATION OF FAILURE

J-ZONE

OLD MAID ENTERTAINMENT
CAMBRIA HEIGHTS, NEW YORK

For information:
Old Maid Entertainment, P.O. Box 110524,
Cambria Heights, NY 11411.

Further information can be obtained online at: www.govillaingo.com

Cover Design & Layout: James Blackwell
www.blackwellspace.com
twitter: @jzanaught

Cover photography and photos on title page, p. 120, p.131, p.156, p. 187, and p. 192 by Alexander Richter.
www.alexanderrichterphoto.com

Copy Editing: Sam Slaughter and James Blackwell

ISBN: 978-0615532271
LCCN: 2011937915

For my grandfather, Arnold Sr., whose book was never published. For my grandfather, Herbie, who I wish had written a book. Your memories live on.

CHAPTER INDEX

0. Foreword: By Chairman Jeff Mao   I

1. The Foundation: Root for the Villain   5

PART ONE: A MUSICAL JOURNEY

2. Darlene   15

3. Epiphany   19

4. Raised by Wolves   23

5. Sucker DJ   35

6. A Bugged Out Day At Power Play   41

7. Man vs. Machines   45

8. Chairman of the Board   51

9. Music for Tu Madre: A Lesson In Self-Preservation   61

10. Legal Action From a Pimp   69

11. Don't Holla! No, Never, Goodbye   73

12. Frequent Flyer Miles   81

13. The Chitlin' Circuit   87

14. Rise & Slip   93

15. The Quitter   101

16. Superheroes & Peers   107

PART TWO: I SMELL BULLSHIT!

17. Back on the Plantation   115

18. Go Go Gadget Ho!   125

19. The Grown Folks' Playground   133

20. Another Wasted Night   139

21. Out for the Count   153

22. A Broad Abroad   161

23. Are Men the New Women (What The Fuck)?   167

PART THREE: WORD TO THE NERD

24. Adventures in Diggin'   173

25. I'm Not An Ex-Con, I Just Like Tapes   183

26. Funky Granny   189

0. FOREWORD:
by Chairman Jeff Mao

I first became aware of the human hip-hop tornado known as J-Zone towards the end of the last century, when his *Music For Tu Madre* EP showed up unsolicited in the mail at Ego Trip corporate HQ. I remember feeling both confused and apprehensive when I first laid eyes on the no-budget record jacket, which featured a slightly blurry, color copied Polaroid of an elderly woman (who I'd later learn was J's grandma) rocking a Champion hoodie and gripping a 40 oz. in one hand while flipping off the camera with the other, her iced grill rugged enough to make the likes of Freddie Foxxx cower in a corner and go knock-kneed.

I promptly put the record aside, ignoring it for several months.

In due time, though, I would get around to listening to J-Zone's music (at the prompting of one of our associates in common, who assured me that the guy was on the up and up and not just, as the English say, "taking the piss"), and I realized how much I'd been snoozing. No, J-Zone wasn't the illest rapper. In fact, the way he relished goofing on rap convention and trumpeting his unglamorous po' pimp ethos (a mix of self-clowning wisecracks and straight up chauvinism), he kind of sounded more like someone's obnoxious kid brother practicing stand-up than any traditional sort of emcee. His beats were funky. But not in the Kool & the Gang *Live at the Sex Machine* sense; more in the ancient school sense of being overtly grubby (not to be confused with grimy) — albeit inventively so, having been resourcefully pieced together from snippets of dollar bin easy listening records, foreign pop tunes, vintage sitcom and film dialog swiped via VHS off the Zenith, and other sampled spare parts.

Nope, J-Zone wasn't your typical rap artist. That was the point. He was the consummate hip-hop misfit — smart yet ign'ant, middle class yet too broke to ball out, a born n' bred New Yorker who worshiped shit-talking Westside playas like Suga Free and Too $hort. I became a fan and began regularly writing up J's records in my "Chairman's Choice" magazine column. (I still maintain that *Pimps Don't Pay Taxes*, his 2001 LP and acknowledged opus, is as historically relevant as any Kanye West or Dipset release from that decade

I

in chronicling rap's evolution from staunchly '90s-style "skills"-reliant sensibili-ties to more fundamentally personality-driven ones.) In this ornery loser, we fellow misfits recognized a kindred spirit. One of us. Folks for whom the Todd Shaw-endorsed maxim "Get in where you fit in" didn't do a damn bit of good 'cause we didn't quite fit in anywhere, and we knew it.

The book you now hold in your hands (or are gazing at via the Kindle, or are being read to aloud by your own personal book-bot, or are having main-lined into the right side of your skull, or whatever the hell format books are published and consumed in by the time this goes public...) is as much the realization of J-Zone's curmudgeonly creative talents as any of his record-ings as an artist and producer. (He's since retired from the game after one too many excruciating, spirit-crushing setbacks – details in the pages that fol-low.) If you're questioning the relevance of a book written by someone who by record industry standards was a commercial failure, well, there's probably a really swell Tyler Perry film novelization somewhere out there that's more your speed. In this fine collection of autobiographical essays and think pieces – which touch on everything from the absurdity of the music industry to gadgetry and social media's suffocation of New York nightlife to questionable fashion trends and gender (several of these musings conveniently located in the sec-tion entitled "I Smell Bullshit") – we have a hip-hop-informed referendum on all the dumb shit that threatens to ruin our existences on this earth one annoying episode at a time.

True, the cynicism of J's tone can reach levels of unmatched nit-picky-ism. (After reading his rant on unwelcome text messages and the charges that add up on his cell phone bill I've made it a policy to only text him in response to a text of his, or be prepared to hand over a pocket of loose change as a penance the next time I see him.) He's a frugal motherfucker, for sure, as evidenced by the "New York State Testing Program – September 2005" binder that he "borrowed" from his old day job to house the manuscript he gave me. It's printed in a font that I think was discontinued some time when he was in middle school. Half the chapters are barely legible – outputted extra light in order to save money on printer toner. I divulge these details not to ridicule him, but because they actually collectively represent one of the characteristics I respect most about J-Zone. He's a D.I.Y. dude till the end. Which honestly makes him as hip-hop as anybody you can name. He don't want nobody to give him nothin'. Open up the door. He'll get it himself. (Do you hear him?)

The other irony in all of this? J-Zone the rapper, as it turns out, is a better and more informed writer than most so-called rap journalists or bloggers that'll infect your eye and mind space. The guy knows how to tell a story, com-

II

pose a lucid argument, and present a well-defined perspective. He's brutally and refreshingly honest with himself in ways cats in hip-hop are conditioned precisely not to be. And truth be told, beneath the cynicism there's genuine heartfelt emotion (peep the book's opening acknowledgements of family mentors if you don't believe me). If he's indeed done making music and has turned his attention to writing, our professional field just got a little stronger.

I just don't know if I have the heart to tell J his latest career move places him at perhaps the lowest point imaginable on the rap food chain. Even a so-called "failed" rapper collects more props than the most respected hip-hop book author. Oh well. He'll figure it out.

– "Chairman" Jeff(erson) Mao, ego trip NYC

1. THE FOUNDATION: ROOT FOR THE VILLAIN

A sizable number of black folks in New York City in the 1960s had the same ideal dream sequence: Harlem, The Bronx, or Brooklyn, to select neighborhoods in Queens, Westchester County, or Long Island. For those unfamiliar with New York's demographics before Brooklyn crack houses became vintage clothing boutiques twenty years down the line, that migration meant bus passes to Bentleys. A hard-working black man was often stacking his earnings and just getting by while he watched modest and diverse public housing transmogrify into downtrodden cauldrons of chaos. His drive to move up and out eventually initiated white flight from many of NYC's outskirt enclaves with one gator shoe, while it mashed the gas pedal of an 8-track equipped Cadillac Brougham with the other.

Buying a house in Southeast Queens in the 1960s was *making it*. Just about all of the neighborhoods of the greater Jamaica region were becoming blue collar utopias for blacks: Hollis, St. Albans, Springfield Gardens, Cambria Heights, Rochdale, Laurelton, and parts of South Jamaica. While a good portion of the region's newcomers included the likes of musicians and entertainers - John Coltrane, Lena Horne, James Brown, Count Basie, Ella Fitzgerald, Milt Hinton, and countless others called the area home - most of the new mortgage holders were 15-hour-day-working, no-shit-taking men, who usually had a calcium-fortified backbone in a wife who endured the ups and downs with them. These folks were a breed that began to taper towards the turn of the century with the advent of crack and reality TV aspirations. Arnold P. Mumford Sr. and Herbie Sheppard, my grandfathers, were card-carrying members of that black brigade.

Arnold Sr., a dark-skinned brother from New Orleans, was the brightest, toughest, and most benevolent person I've ever known. Although he had been through the Second World War, the depression, and the racial wringer, he didn't curse. In fact, when the distributor cap on his ride blew up in his face while he was amidst of one of his several unsuccessful D.I.Y. improvement projects, he never uttered any four letter words besides "ouch." He was a non-stop joker, yet his tolerance for bullshit was lilliputian.

The average trip on Southeast Queens' Q113 bus route was and still is eerily reminiscent of the bus ride featured in Method Man's "Bring the Pain" video - thuggish, crowded, and a valley girl's nightmare. Arnold Sr. once boldly told a group of rowdy 113-riding hoodlums to stop cursing in the presence of the ladies on the bus. At a time when half of the hardheads in neighborhood had burners stashed under their sheepskin coats, the Q113 patrons went mute quicker than Cleveland Cavs owner Dan Gilbert could say "nigger" when LeBron James took his talents to South Beach. The quip "let me go get my strap" was to Arnold Sr. what "Dynomite!" was to J.J. Evans, and his jovial nature evaporated in a nanosecond when you didn't do what was supposed to be done. The average man is dual-natured, but there was another level of dichotomy with Arnold Sr. that puzzled the hell out of me.

On one hand, he was a devout Catholic who took me to Sunday mass sessions at the local church and made me memorize The Ten Commandments as a fourth grader. On the other, his still unpublished book (bluntly titled, *Dear White Folks*) took a brute swipe at the white Anglo-Saxon view of the world, the same view that was the Duracell in the ass-backwards religion he followed. *Dear White Folks* was one of Arnold Sr.'s few avenues to release steam, but today its handwritten manuscript still rests peacefully in a blue binder next to a VCR instruction booklet in my attic. A portrait of a white as a golf ball Jesus hung above his bed, but he lay on that same Sealy Tempurpedic mentally preparing his notes for *Dear White Folks*. The inability to place him neatly into a box showed me early in my life that contradictory behavior confuses people, but it's what ultimately makes a man intriguing.

Arnold Sr. and his wife, Edith (aka "Evil E"), jettisoned their lives in New Orleans for New York (specifically, The Bronx) in 1947. After popping out two sons less than a year apart (my father being the eldest), the family relocated to Brooklyn's notorious Ingersoll (aka "Fort Greene") Housing Projects. A working class, 1950s Fort Greene didn't start the groundwork on its crime-spiked reputation until the '60s, which was around the time a stray bullet ricocheted its way through the Mumford's living room window and lodged itself in a couch that was occupied 15 minutes prior.

"Y'all hurry up and pack your things, we're moving to Queens," Arnold Sr. said with zero warning to the family one day in 1964. In October of that year, he bought the modest one family home in the Rochdale section of South Jamaica, Queens that I live in today for $17,000.

Herbie "Pop Pop" Sheppard, my grandfather on my mother's side of the family, was also a book worthy character. He'd be the life of the party when in his comfort zone, which often featured Harry Belafonte albums and jokes. However, he'd become engulfed in seriousness and paranoia when betrayed. Also a war vet, Herbie always kept some well-oiled ammunition in the stash in case of emergency. When someone went and fucked up, he wore a piercing ice grill facial expression like a $3,000 seersucker suit. A spitting image of that ominous glare makes a cameo whenever I get pissed off today.

A brown-skinned, hazel-eyed man with family roots in Barbados and the brother of a Tuskegee Airman, Herbie was under constant pressure and withstood bullshit at every turn. The general consensus from what I could gather as a kid was that the adults in my family thought he was evil. In retrospect, I feel that consensus was extremely unjust. So what he almost peeled my cranium like a tangerine for reaching for a second glass of orange juice at the table when I was seven? Yes, he had enough artillery in the basement of his Cambria Heights home to use it as a stage set for an episode of *M*A*S*H*. True, his mile long hit list - which included everyone from his 90-year-old, slow-moving Creole mother-in-law to a host of public figures and politicians - was hung meticulously near his superior firepower with not one single solitary typo. As I aged though, I began to see Herbie as my own personal hero, an oft misunderstood man who simply had a low threshold for bullshit.

Herbie shared a house with five women at one point. For fuck's sake, could the man ever get a break? Trying to hit on five different broads in a bar in one night with all of their different idiosyncrasies would give me a God damn aneurysm. Herbie never threw a Molotov cocktail into a nail salon while living under those circumstances, so that meant that he was probably the most mild-mannered brother who ever paced the planet. He and his wife raised their four daughters in Brooklyn and Roosevelt (Long Island), before moving to Cambria Heights at the close of the 1960s.

Herbie's eldest daughter met my father at St. John's University during summer class sessions in 1970. My father had a rough go trying to pull my studious and quirky mother at first. It tends to be a struggle when you're spraying pimponomics at her friend simultaneously. Nonetheless, the unlikely pair was married in three years. Three years after that - somewhere between Don Cornelius interviewing BT Express on *Soul Train* and George Jefferson kicking Tom Willis out of his apartment on *The Jeffersons* - they conceived me. On my father's 29th birthday, I made my world debut in The Bronx's Albert Einstein Hospital as a complicated and hard to categorize mash-up of both families in both appearance and personality.

The root of my physical appearance is a mix of Herbie's hazel eyes and facial features, my mother's light skin, and Arnold Jr.'s nappy hair. To this day, people in the street stare at me like I took a dump on a baking sheet, placed it in their oven, and turned it on 425.

Yo man, what the fuck are you?

The first time I heard that question that in the smart aleck tone that I usually hear it in, it was from a kid on some playground in the 1980s. In response, I tried my best to make an origami crane out of his neck. Thirty years later, the torch is carried by everyone from strangers in the street to women on dating websites. These days though, I respond to the continuous racial quizzing in a manner more civil.

I'm a black man who looks different and lives in America, and despite everyone's favorite liberal slogan ("race doesn't matter to me"), I can't escape questioning. It's pretty hilarious to watch people fidget with me upon our initial meeting, as they nervously feel for an opening in the conversation to spring race questions into the mix. It's even funnier when folks think I'm lying or my answer determines the direction our conversation goes from that point forward. My Caribbean and Louisiana Black Creole roots give me a look that's caused me to spend the last 34 years fielding racial inquiries from bizarre white folks I barely know, who place their forearms next to mine to do the "complexion comparison" in their quest to gauge my level of "blackness" and cross-examine my claims. Then there are the apprehensive black folks, who can usually tell I'm black, but triple-take before giving me a nod. Of course, Latinos have addressed me speaking Spanish at breakneck speed and look exceedingly perplexed when I answer with a simple "si" and break into a half-assed Bachata dance. Everyone else just stares for a long time, before I blurt out, "I'm a Pisces."

It's also a trip watching people attempt to decode me while looking at me and listening to me speak. If I ditch the hood slang and opt for using solid grammar on that particular day, it fucks them up.

"You don't even sound black," a fan of my music once told me. I guess I can see where he was coming from. Not too many brothers will get on a record and rap about being in a pussy drought and jerking off in an elevator for blue ball relief. Self-deprecation generally isn't embraced in the black community. Nonetheless, when folks audition for roles in these behavioral shit shows via ignorance, they give me one huge advantage - they make it a fuck of a lot easier to weed them out quickly. Weeding out people I don't like in an expeditious manner damn near makes me come, so now I embrace the strange human behavior that my appearance generates.

*T*he root of my attitude comes from Herbie's misunderstood curmudgeon and Arnold Sr.'s yin and yang. Those two men lent their personalities to my young Play-Doh mind.

I've spent 34 years around people, some of whom were memorable for their astounding greatness, but most of whom were memorable for being bullshit. Therefore, I make no bones about saying that I generally dislike people. Part of *Root for the Villain* is my personal rampage against bullshit, the absurdities of mankind, and the general stupidity of people, both in the music business and in everyday life. I truly feel that the ghost of Herbie is wielding the remote control and guiding me on my rampage.

As J-Zone the musician, the 21 people who actually knew who I was didn't know whether to identify with my seriousness for my craft or my foul-mouthed, silly, and misogynistic persona. As J-Zone the writer and personality, people don't know whether to identify with the messages at the core, or the acerbic, over the top, and cantankerous wrapping paper I deliver them in.

ArnOLd Sr.

I hate ignorance with an unwavering passion, yet my fascination with "ign'ant" rap music - a sub-genre rife with bitch-bashing, senseless violence, and knucklehead-isms - ran deeply enough within me to inspire my monthly magazine column solely dedicated to it. I've been told I'm too straight-laced and straightforward to succeed in the entertainment world, but too eccentric and rebellious to survive in a nine-to-five. A woman will often wonder what type of man I am to sing along to Too $hort's "Blowjob Betty" while I ride around in the car with her on a date. Then again, I treat this girl better than her ex-man who brought her flowers and ser-

herbie

9

enaded her with bullshit love songs did, so she doesn't know whether to dump me or hump me. As many galaxies apart as our values and beliefs are, I truly believe the ghost of Arnold Sr. is puppeteer behind the ambiguous behavior itself.

While bullshit has played an Oscar-winning role as my primary nemesis and being difficult to figure out has aided me in finding clarity in the world around me, failure has played a unique role in my life as well. We're all subject to failure, but I've learned to deal with failure by finding humor in it.

Success is relative to how you look at things, and some days I view my journey as a success. Nonetheless, after 15 years of tireless work in the music business, critical acclaim, and respect from a wide range of notable musicians (from hip-hop legends to current pop stars), I was told by a publisher that I should "become a success some other way before attempting to publish a book, because you haven't been successful enough for people to care about your stories and opinions." The chick who told me that has a point. My most successful album has sold about 12,000 units to date (since its release in 2001). Who the fuck am I to be writing a book?

We live in a world of tangible results, so in terms of acquiring major money and fame, I've undoubtedly failed. When it comes to dealing with people for any extended period of time, I can claim a D average and that's only because I actually put up an effort at one point. My drop back into the nine-to-five world after being encapsulated by the entertainment world for so long has been a free-falling and bumpy one at best. My Too $hort-inspired misogynistic karaoke routines on dates are a sign that I've failed miserably (albeit hilariously) when it comes to romancing the opposite sex. My vehement adverse reactions to all things current and popular are proof that I've failed to find my spot in the modern world. My soul is still stuck in 1990 and it's only reachable by smoke signal.

It's a fact that sometimes you have to "play the game" in order to be successful. You know, just suck it up and play by the rules to get what you want. If the rules of the game are bullshit and the players are wasting my time, I'd rather not play the game at all and celebrate in the face of failure. I own up to every victory and loss I've endured with the same volume, because no matter the result, I usually evaded playing the game.

Back at the ranch, the hero plays by the rules and makes sure the photographer only gets his good side. When he fails, he hides like a bitch. He either winds up being the clean cut community leader who got busted with dope or the bohemian slam poet who preached all that dreck about how misogyny is ruining hip-hop, but he has 12 kids by 12 different women. They're both as contradictory and prone to failure as I am, but they'll never cheese for the cameras with the drugs in hand or all 12 baby mamas in tow like I would.

This collection of memoirs and rants is an extremely opinionated and niche-based ride. Although I hope it conjures up discussion, debate, and most importantly, laughs, I made it for myself and the few hundred people roaming the globe who are like me. If it doesn't sell and nobody cares, fuck it, my records and CDs pay stabilized rent in cut out bins anyway. So what do my stories and opinions mean to the average American? Not much, but I don't give a fuck about the average American. The average American reads *The DaVinci Code* or *Rich Dad, Poor Dad*.

This book was done with limited resources at every turn. Upon its completion, I was asked by family and friends about its availability in Barnes & Noble and the chances of it selling a significant amount of units. You're more likely to find a copy of *Root for the Villain* in a prison library than in Barnes & Noble. If I sell 500 copies of this thing, I'm a best-seller in the world of J-Zone.

How I look, the way I was raised, and what I've experienced have all contributed to what *Root for the Villain* is and how it was done. Testing people's sense of humor, challenging their intelligence, throwing a victory party while staring failure in the face, being contrary and somewhat contradictory, and calling out bullshit without an iota of concern for popular opinion - as an artist and personality, that list of semi-dysfunctional attributes has been my trademark. So for the small handful of J-Zone fans still roaming the globe who appreciate that approach, this book is for you.

I'm also using this book as a platform to be the spokesman for all other good-hearted people who somehow got sick of people in general along the way - this book is for you. If you were entrenched in record store bins or religiously watching *Yo! MTV Raps* in 1990, this book is for you. If you feel lost in the cryptic world of internet acronyms and digitized smiley faces made with semi-colons, this book is for you. If you felt that Snoop Dogg deserved an Oscar for his role as Rodney in *Baby Boy* or believe Mitch "Blood" Green belongs on a postage stamp, this book is for you. If your port of entry into adulthood featured Reaganomics, African medallions, CD long boxes made of cardboard, and the Rodney King beating video, this book is for you.

Lastly, I dedicate this to the memory of my real deal grandfathers, Arnold P. Mumford Sr. and Herbie Sheppard. The former refused to be put into a box and the latter spent most of his days being tested and misunderstood. Not a day goes by where I don't look at my own life, wonder what they would do if

11

they were in my shoes, and give them a nod in Real OG heaven. Thank you sirs for guiding me through my daily excursions, this book is for you.

Part One:
A Musical Journey

performing with cee-lo (2006)

turning up the volume (1981)

2. DARLENE

I find it funny that a female hip-hop personality I've never met initiated my realization of sex. All you had to say to any male rap fan circa 1989 was "Darlene". The mere sound of her name was like taking a Viagra pill. If it still didn't ring a bell, all you had to say was, "Ice-T's girlfriend, the chick on his album covers."

Ice-T was one of the first rappers I ever became a fan of. He was "light-skinded" like me, and Darlene was quite possibly the finest female specimen west of Pluto. A startling vixen with a body worth foreclosure on your home, I discovered her standing scantily clad and holding a shot gun on Ice's "High Rollers" 12" single album cover while I was standing with a rock-hard bone in a record store in New Rochelle, NY.

I had stumbled into Records Unlimited on that particular Saturday afternoon in the spring of '89 to find a few songs I'd heard on my favorite video show. My newly budding interest in rap music was planted primarily by *Yo! MTV Raps*, with hosts Ed Lover, Dr. Dre, and Fab 5 Freddy. The show was MTV's attempt to bring rap videos into living rooms across America. I realized that their attempt was working when one of the snow-whitest preppy girls in my junior high school ran up to me in gym class and quoted a line from ultra-Afrocentric rapper King Sun.

"Yo man, you gotta be black!" she kept blurting out while we were running laps around the gym. "King Sun!"

The show had aired videos for Kid N' Play's "Rollin with Kid N' Play," Boogie Down Productions' "Jack of Spades," the Jungle Brothers' "Straight Out the Jungle" and my new favorite, "High Rollers," earlier in the week. I had no idea that thumbing through the Ice-T section at the record store would change my life forever. When I flipped over the record cover, I damn near spilled on myself. Any man who would've remained faithful to his wife when crossed with the opportunity for a night with Darlene just wasn't a man, and to this day, I still say the "High Rollers" 12" was the greatest $4 purchase I've ever made. Musically, it wasn't too shabby either. Ice had me locked in on the first line:

Speed of light, fast

It's like walkin' barefoot over broken glass.

Rap was my new shit, and for the first time in my life, my favorite song of the moment wasn't a '70s funk song that nobody cared about anymore. Ice-T's rhyme style was compelling and the music was lifted from a funky Edwin Starr joint that I had in my record collection. But long after the needle slid through the final grooves of "High Rollers," I would sit there holding the cover, salivating over Darlene. I was 12 years old and just beginning to notice females in school, but at a time when our food wasn't yet packed with growth hormones, none of the girls in school had anything "back there" or "up there" yet.

My crush on Darlene became so intense, that daydreaming about her in seventh grade math class caused me to pitch a tent once. I had made the mistake of wearing a nylon sweat suit to school that day, so when I needed to piss like an elephant, I had to stay seated until my flying flag went down. All this shit I heard in math class about Pi equaling 3.14 was bullshit; Darlene equaled 10 out of 10.

puberty, darlene style

About a month into the seventh grade, Darlene and I finally met in my school gymnasium, alone. There were no words exchanged, just a passionate round of kissing. I dropped my gym shorts to reveal a baby stick of dynamite. Just as quickly as Darlene jumped on me, it was all over. By the time I gathered myself and looked around, it was a seasonally cool Saturday morning in October; I was sprawled out on my bed with strange gooey stuff all over the front hole of my favorite pajamas. A glimpse at my sheets revealed more spots.

"I broke my dick!" I screamed in a panic, probably loud enough for my mother to hear me.

I only used profanity twice in my life before I was 13 years old - the time my grandparents and I flipped over in the family Cadillac on the Clearview Expressway in Queens and that autumn morning, when I woke up from my first wet dream. After about five minutes of pandemonium and thinking I'd never be able to piss again, I recalled Mike from science class telling me he had a wet dream over the summer. I calmed down a bit and attempted to clean up the mess, but the water just made things worse. When I discovered that my mother wasn't home, I also busted my first ever load of laundry. I grabbed some quarters and the laundry room key off the foyer table, a bottle of Tide out of the garage, and scurried to delete the evidence. Darlene owes me $3 in quarters.

Repeat faux sexual episodes starring Robin Givens, Jasmine Guy, Vanity, and all of them at once played out over the next few months, making me a pro at doing laundry and cleaning up evidence. I always got a kick out of knowing that quite possibly, I had experienced the very first hip-hop themed nocturnal emission in history. Adolescence had arrived, and this new rap thing was partially ushered into my life by the incomparable Darlene. I had no clue that rap wouldn't be merely a passing phase, but the soundtrack to my formative years and my eventual career path. Judging by the earlier part of the decade though, trying my hand at a rap career didn't appear feasible.

17

3. EPIPHANY

Rap was a mere blip on my radar in the early 1980s, but so was everything else the majority of kids my age liked. That included GI Joes, Transformers, Thunder-cats, Garbage Pail Kids, Gobots, and other useless '80s kid rigmarole. I had short video game phases with the Atari 2600 and the Nintendo, but they didn't stick. Back then, if you saved the bitch in a one minute game of *Donkey Kong* or busted the pterodactyl on his beak in boards five, nine, and thirteen in a game of *Joust* on the 2600, the game was basically over. I gave up on video games completely when I found out that you could skip all of the boxers and get right to Mike Tyson with a special code when playing *Punch Out!* I was a late bloomer with sports and my initial interest in a hip-hop lifestyle faded two weeks after I nearly croaked while trying to break dance in 1985.

"Man, Run-DMC is the best shit out, 'Sucker MCs' is fresh!"

It was Rob from upstairs, one of the few other black kids in our working class apartment complex that was surrounded by wealth and in a predominantly white town in Westchester County. My folks had vacated Queens to get away from my grandparents and neighborhoods that were being pillaged by crime and a few years later, a nuclear bomb named crack. The 180 degree change was one with better schools and safer streets, plus it gave me the advantage of being raised between two neighborhoods that were as polar opposite as one could possibly find within a 24-mile radius. Weekly treks over the Throgs Neck Bridge to go back to Queens balanced the 'fly in the buttermilk' experience I was enduring at Central Elementary School, where Rob and I did our best to keep up with the new shit.

"Yo, you gotta listen to this song! He says, 'Drive a big car, get your gas from Getty!'"

I credit Rob for introducing me to rap. For a good six months, I was hyped on it. My pops took us to see *Breakin' 2: Electric Boogaloo* at Whitestone Cinemas in the Bronx. Soon after, our mothers brought us to Caldor's Department Store in Port Chester to buy copies of the *NYC Breakers* compilation tape. A week later, I almost broke my ribs doing The Worm on Rob's living room floor. Trying to emulate Turbo in *Breakin' 2* was an inane waste of time with me being the chubby bastard that I was, and my break dancing accident caused me to bury my interest in all things rap-related for another five years.

As an only child with a giant afro that always had a pick stuck in it, I shifted my focus to funk fantasies. It was only right; I was delivered by Dr. Coolidge Abel-Bay, the financial backer for '70s funk bands B.T. Express and Brass Construction. Combing through the record collections of relatives, I unearthed albums by Kool & the Gang, Slave, James Brown, and Funkadelic. My immediate goal was to start my own funk band, even though Jheri curls, electric drums, key-tars, and love ballads had long since replaced funk by 1987. I may have been the only 10-year-old in the Western Hemisphere who was spending his Saturday afternoons in old record stores. My folks had divorced in the early part of the decade, so my father would take me on weekends and leave me in Greenline Records in Jamaica, Queens for hours at a time to blow my allowance money on old vinyl.

I stayed with my grandparents in Queens on weekends. After sitting in the basement with my bass guitar and emulating the basslines on the records, I'd come upstairs and pick Arnold Sr.'s encyclopedia-like brain about everything from the periodic table of elements to the origins of *Soul Train*. When he was sure I had learned something for the day, we'd kick back and watch *227* and *Amen*, two black '80s TV sitcoms that came on back to back. I'd sit there mesmerized as I zeroed in on the titties of Sandra Clark (played by Jackee Harry) on *227* bopping up and down and her big round ass sliding from side to side like an ink cartridge in a printer. Had I hit puberty in 1987, she would've been a suitable replacement for Darlene.

In my grandparents' weekend and school break efforts to mold me into a devout Catholic, they enrolled me in a heat-less and crumbling Sunday School on Farmers Blvd. in Springfield Gardens, Queens for a four year Confirmation campaign. Tremaine was my lone classmate the first year; he would snap on me every week.

"Nigga, why you listen to all that old shit?" he would always ask with a laugh. "This nigga LL Cool J is stoopid def! You need to cut that 'fro too, shit is out."

It was almost like it bothered my friends that we had nothing in common. Rob and Tremaine were older and already checking for chicks. They listened to rap and contemporary R&B, sported waves and fades in their hair, and dressed in the freshest Benetton gear. I was still wearing shit my grandmother bought me from Alexander's department store and looking like a young and high-yellow Lamont Sanford.

When police officer Ed Byrne was ambushed in a parked car not too far from my grandparent's house (Arnold Sr. later wrote NYC Mayor Ed Koch a letter expressing his displeasure with the city naming 91st Avenue after the fallen cop), Southeast Queens was at the pinnacle of a war with the crack epidemic. Koch set a heat-seeking missile on area drug dealers; the entire area became a war zone. People were hostages on their own blocks in some places. Herbie basically said, "Fuck all this"; in late '87, he loaded his ammunition into a U-Haul truck and abandoned Cambria Heights for Virginia.

Even in much wealthier Westchester, crack made a cameo. The Larchmont Motel, which was adjacent to my district middle school, became low-income housing. The drugs, poverty, and routine violence at the motel became a concern for parents whose kids had to walk past it to get home everyday. Nancy Reagan apparently wasn't getting enough dick at the White House, because she launched a "Just Say No!" to drugs campaign that seemed fatuous to me even at age 11. Her ploy was brilliantly aimed at inner-city kids who went to school and learned about what queer-looking white guys in wigs did 200 years ago by day and watched their older brothers sell crack and purchase *Back To the Future*-esque Marty McFly rides by night. Gotcha Nancy!

I remember my family being incensed at the Howard Beach racial attack in 1986. I also remember Meech (a friend of mine who lived in the motels) and I getting ready stomp the shit out of Gary, a white kid, for laughing about it at Central School.

Meanwhile, my funk idols had since turned to activator-slick R&B and mastered the art of making bad comeback records to support illegitimate kids from their sexcapades of the '70s. Rap was the only genre of music that was fully addressing all of the insanity that was going down in America circa 1988, but I didn't know it. Arnold Sr. never let me roam around the Rochdale area to hear it pulsating out of car stereos and there wasn't much to hear at Central School, so I began to draw fictional album covers with myself on them sporting a big 'fro and playing my bass guitar. By the time I hit fifth grade, I was waist deep in funk records that nobody seemed to care about anymore, or so I thought.

Rob and my man Sean from the Valley section of the Northeast Bronx constantly put the pressure on me to stop looking like a young member of Lakeside and get with the new shit that other young black kids were listening to.

"Just watch *Yo! MTV Raps*, trust me," they would both plead.

In early 1989, I obliged out of boredom. EPMD's "You Gots to Chill" video came on, and when I heard Kool & the Gang's "Jungle Boogie" playing over Zapp's "More Bounce to the Ounce" in perfect unison, I was hooked. I couldn't figure out how the fuck they did it. The 1985 rap production method of synthetic drum machine boom giving way to sampling was the progression that piqued my interest, because what was being made of the records I was studying was funkier than the records themselves. Other people did in fact give a shit about the funk records I was running into the ground, but instead of emulating the basslines, they were straight lifting them to make new music.

By the time I hit middle school, it was more than just an ongoing game of *Name That Funk Tune*. I began to realize that everything going on in the world was being dissed, discussed, and dissected by rap music. The sheer boldness and attitude of it all drew me in the way Hulk Hogan and George Michael captivated the majority of my classmates. My 12-year-old brain was now ready to absorb and apply, as I began to get a hard dick throughout the day for no reason and question everything around me.

I finally adopted the fashion too, pissing all my boys off when I got my hi-top fade haircut without "paying dues" (growing it for months from a short haircut).

"You already had a 'fro man, that's cheating!" my boy Ivan spat at me. Bern-Ski the Barber cut a crisp 7 inch flattop out of my 'fro and I came out of Al's Barber Shop in New Rochelle looking like Kid from Kid N' Play after 30 minutes in the chair. My mother put her inimitable arts and crafts skills to use by making me a polka dot shirt so I could look like Kwame, an ultra-stylish rapper who built his career image primarily on his trademark dotted shirts.

After a year though, a seemingly innocuous fad (in the eyes of my mother) went awry. I stopped wearing polka dots, because only punks wore those shits by 1990. I stopped doing my doofy version of the Running Man dance at school functions, because of what I heard Ice Cube say in a song:

> *I don't wanna see no dancin', I'm sick of that shit!*

I abandoned jovial rap in search of something with more meat, something to coincide with my adolescent-like adverse reactions to everything well-behaved and innocent. It was also a matter of survival.

4. RAISED BY WOLVES

The summer of 1990 was when it all went downhill. Darlene had already introduced me to the pleasures of a nut, I was getting old enough to smell bullshit, and I was getting my ass handed to me in snap sessions at school. Junior high was a bit more of a mixed bag than Central, so I befriended other black students from the other district feeder elementary schools. The kids in my new posse were a bit more street smart than I was. When they got to snapping on mamas and each other's inability to get some pussy, I was a sweet target. With no siblings to show me the ropes, I always got rat-packed by the crew when it came time to play the dozens. Even the kids at my Sunday school began to snap, and Jamaica, Queens kids made some of the baddest muthafuckas in my junior high look like Paul Pfeiffer from *The Wonder Years*.

Adolescence is comparable to a six year bid in jail. You have to manage to stay the right course, but still break your foot off in someone's ass in the mess hall every now and then to let them know that you won't be punked. I took one loss too many at the end of the seventh grade. On the last day of school I got barbecued by the crew so viciously, I came home crying like a sucker. They even broke the "Homie Code" and slayed me in front of chicks. I knew a Joe Clark level of action was needed, and pronto.

Every rap tape released in 1990 that sported the newly-introduced Parental Advisory: Explicit Lyrics sticker was bought and studied. If a tape didn't have a warning sticker, it meant that it was soft, so I didn't bother. The only notable exceptions to the "sticker rule" that I can remember were Eric B. & Rakim's *Let the Rhythm Hit 'Em*, A Tribe Called Quest's debut album, and L.L. Cool J's *Mama Said Knock You Out*.

My new training regimen fed me a steady rap diet of insults, boasts, cusswords, misogyny, anger, sexual conquests, homophobia, humor, black pride, and knowledge. I also began to listen to my dad's old adult comedy records late at night with the headphones on, so my mother couldn't hear the signifyin', jive talkin', and non-stop cussin' being pumped into my brain through a Sony syringe. Rudy Ray Moore (aka Dolemite), Richard Pryor, and Eddie Murphy routines stole my attention when I got too bad for *The Cosby Show*. I realized then how much Black comedy and early '90s rap had in common -

both were immensely entertaining and provided 20 pounds of shit-talking in a 10 pound bag, but both also represented different eras of black America and had underlying messages at hand. More importantly, both possessed what I wasn't getting enough of listening to funk, being an only child in a single parent household, and going to school in a place where I was an outsider - ammunition for crafting my own persona.

Mom dukes wouldn't let me attend a then very young DJ Pete Rock's parties at New Rochelle High School that Rob always told me about. New Rochelle-Mount Vernon beef had become so thick in the late '80s, that people were leaving those jams on stretchers. Arnold Sr. wouldn't allow me to attend parties in the Rochdale Village housing complex across the street from my house in Queens, either. Nonetheless, I found other ways to get my fix.

Between video shows and DJs like *Yo! MTV Raps*, *Video Music Box*, DJ Red Alert, and DJ Chuck Chillout, I captured it all on VHS, taped it on cassette, and wrote it down. I'd hit up the Music Factory on 165th Street near the Coliseum Mall in Jamaica and buy whatever my now $20 a week allowance could afford. Either The Wiz or Tower Records on Central Ave. in Yonkers were my Westchester spots. When money got low, I went to the Black Expo fairs at the Jacob Javits Center or 125th Street in Harlem with my mother to buy bootleg tapes for $5 each from the peddlers. I was customizing the "new me" based on bits and pieces of what I was hearing, like some deranged cut and paste mad biologist. By the time eighth grade rolled around in September, I went looking for muthafuckas to pin my jive talk on. I even added a plethora of four-letter words and ruthless mama jokes to my arsenal; bring it on, cocksucker.

I doubt rappers like Audio 2, Grand Daddy IU, The Afros, and No Face knew (or cared) that they were shaping some teenager's personality somewhere. But the way I saw it, I was being raised by a pack of rap wolves and their songs defined a good chunk of my personal development, for better or worse.

The Afros' "Hoecakes" and No Face's "Fake Hair Wearing Bitch"

With Run-DMC's popularity declining in 1990, DJ Jam Master Jay delved into side projects like The Afros. One of the members of the group was DJ Hurricane, the Beastie Boys' DJ. The Afros rapped about five things: afros, hoes, jail, bank robberies, and New York Knick games. Also from Hollis, Queens and under the Def Jam/RAL umbrella was No Face, a group that could only be fairly described as a hip-hop take on Blowfly. No Face also had a heavy allegiance to Ed Lover from *Yo! MTV Raps* and both groups were extremely short-lived one album wonders who were quickly tossed into the novelty bin.

I was one of eight lucky winners of a rap trivia contest given in *Serious Hip-Hop* (a Washington DC-based and equally short lived magazine), in which the prize was a copy of No Face's *Wake Your Daughter Up* cassette. My pops' girlfriend bought me The Afros' *Kickin' Afrolistics* CD for Christmas in 1990. My introduction to misogyny came with that entertaining pair of albums. Both are partially responsible for not only influencing my own rap career, but my first (and only) severe ass-kicking at the hands of a female.

LaTeesha was in the seventh grade, a grade below me. She was my homeboy's little sister and provided the first in a long series of disastrous encounters with the opposite sex. She had a crush on me, but I could give two shits less and the unrequited shows of affection began to boil her blood. She was about 6'1", stronger than I was, and could get extremely ghetto in an eye blink for no apparent reason. Love letters would appear in my locker one day, and then a hate letter would follow when I didn't respond. Those erratic shows of emotion prepped me for many a relationship in adulthood, but at the time, the broad just got on my fuckin' nerves and the funky behavior couldn't be blamed on a menstrual cycle just yet. LaTeesha was a hair in my grits, so I threw some lines from my two favorite albums of the moment at her.

No Face's "Fake Hair Wearing Bitch" (which featured the 2 Live Crew) was a real romantic ditty:

> *Your hair ain't grew from short to long,*
> *is it yours, I have my doubts*
>
> *Your eyes ain't change from brown to blue,*
> *bitch, you need to take the shit out*
> *(Take that shit out!)*
>
> *You always talkin' bout where you been,*

and who you know like I ain't shit

Well you need to shut your fucking mouth,
and just, suck my dick… bitch!

The Afros' mantra of 'fros and hoes lived vividly on "Hoecakes", which also sent me down the good ol' path to bitch baiting:

Just coolin' one evening, depressed
and uptight

So I called up one of my hoes, and told
her to spend the night

Woke up in the morning, after I served
that ass

The ho was hungry, said she wanted some
breakfast (What she want?!)

She wanted eggs, sausage, grits, and bacon
(Hungry ho)

I said yo, ho, you got to be mistaken

Get out my pantry, and put down my
Corn Flakes

Bitch, get a glass of milk, some juice,
and a hoecake!

Chorus (4x):

Hoecakes, hoecakes… Hoecakes for my hoes!
(I'm hungry… please!)

I ran around school delivering those slices of decorum to a lot of girls. Beneath it all, the brash misogyny was my own little decoy for the fact that I was terrified of female rejection. But LaTeesha was the wrong bitch to test them on. After she caught me throwing out the box of chocolates she slipped into my locker on clean-up day, I responded to her anger with a line of pimpishly cool Afro Hoecake wisdom. Bad decision - she went Bonecrusher Smith on me.

"What the fuck you say about my mama, you little punk ass nigga?"

26

I hadn't said anything about her mama. She just felt like fucking me up, so she grabbed me by my hair and proceeded to throw *Rumble in the Jungle*-style uppercuts and Blackbelt Jones roundhouse kicks. One of her kicks actually lifted me off the floor vertically. I somehow broke free and ran to the main office screaming in a petrified, Phillip Bailey falsetto. Unfortunately, that didn't stop the bitch from going in there to continue whoopin' my ass like a world champ. The Assistant Principal finally spared me further humiliation when she separated us. To my chagrin, the lone witnesses to this ass-whoopin' were the two biggest big mouths in the school, Jerry and Little Mike. Even worse, that was merely round one.

"Come here you little ugly, punk ass nigga. Say something so I can fuck you up," she taunted every time I crossed her path. An onomatopoeia solo on my forehead always followed. Smack! Ping! Pop! Boom! Pow! "You faggot."

Batman had nothing on that bitch.

I dealt with this shit from her an average of three times per week for two straight years. I was raised to never hit a female, but something tells me that even if I fought that bitch like a man, she still would've simonized the floor with my face. She eventually got sick of slappin' me around, but the damage to my rep was done; I could never act like a tough guy and be taken seriously. The Afros and No Face owe me $7.50 each to pay for the Miami Dolphins Starter cap that LaTeesha snatched off my head and tossed down a sewer drain.

AUDiO 2: "What ya LOOKiN' At?"

I was too busy listening to funk when Audio 2 dropped the classic "Top Billin" around 1987, but I was on board when they dropped their sophomore record (*I Don't Care - The Album*) in 1990. Seeing a photo of the group circled and crossed out in *The Village Voice* piqued my interest even further. Apparently, Audio 2's flagrantly homophobic rhymes put them on the popular newspaper's shit list. The group's rapper, Milk Dee, was everything I wasn't, but needed to become to get past being the water boy in my crew - arrogant, brash, and obnoxious. I studied *I Don't Care - The Album* from front to back, particularly the songs "Get Your Mother off the Crack" and "What Ya Lookin' At?" The latter sounded particularly rogue, so I laid down the law with volume and recited it in the school hallways:

27

I can't understand why ya lookin this way

What's the matter witcha boy? Are ya gay?!

Yo, I hope that ain't the case

Cause gay muthas, get punched in the face

Word to Giz, I hate faggots

*They livin' in the Village like meat
on some maggots*

I felt like a rebel for calling everyone in school a faggot for two weeks and telling every one from teachers to classmates that I didn't care, but my subscription to the *Audio 2 Guide to Living Correctly* was what initiated "the talk" that parents are supposed to have with their kids.

"So your mother tells me you got in trouble for running around school calling everything a faggot," said my pops nonchalantly, as we nibbled on Big Macs in the Galleria Mall Food Court in White Plains. "Do you even know what faggot means?"

"Yeah man, a nigga that don't want no pussy," I responded like a young Richard Pryor. I guess mentioning pussy caused the floodgates to open, because pops and I then partook in the same 'your dick goes in the girl and nine months later a baby pops out' spiel that Furious Styles and Tre enacted in *Boyz-N-The Hood*. My parents would've been happy to know that the chances of me getting anyone pregnant at that time fluctuated somewhere between 0.1 and 0.2 percent. You can't 'stick your thing in her' when girls think you're a funny-looking pain in the ass.

"I like Audio 2, those are some good beats!"

It was extremely bizarre to hear my 42-year-old father blurt that out in the middle of a dire discussion about my port of entry into manhood. "But you have to know entertainment versus what you can say and do in the real world. Capiche?"

I may have been the only kid with a parent who was actually a rap fan circa 1990, and the fact that pops dealt with issues instead of trying to shelter me from them was probably why I respected his stance. It also made the experience of enjoying the most explicit rap tape without using the lyrics as an instruction manual a much easier job. Milk Dee owes my pops $10 for the two #3 meals from McDonald's that made the riot act easier to deliver.

Gang Starr: "Just To Get a Rep"

My school basketball team played a majority of its games against the near-by Yonkers public schools. By the 1990-91 school year, the city of Yonkers was a fresh four years out of a desegregation lawsuit that came about due to the bizarre and purposely unequal zoning of its housing and public schools. Thus, every school we balled against had a respectable core of "eighth grade" knuckleheads with goatees and gold fronts who could windmill dunk.

"Y'all niggas gonna lose this game, y'all know that right?" threatened one of the players on the Mark Twain Middle School team. He had to be at least 22 years old, because he sold the wolf ticket in a baritone on par with Barry White nursing a cold. We lost by about 80 points that day, then they chased us out of their gym.

The Emerson Middle School team did Mark Twain one better. Emerson rushed our gym looking like a thugged-out posse of Smurfs - baby blue uniforms, matching North Carolina Tarheel Starter jackets and hats, and baby blue Patrick Ewing sneakers that I don't recall ever seeing for sale. If that wasn't enough, their pre-game war call was downright treacherous:

Stick up kids is out to tax!

Fuck. We were about to get robbed in our own school by the visiting team. I knew the menacing phrase from Nice-N-Smooth's song "Funky for You," but they kept chanting it over and over and over again as they trooped into our locker room bopping harder than I've ever seen anyone bop, before or ever since. If bopping cured cancer, those niggas could run 5K marathons in Chernobyl every day for three straight years, come home, bop to the corner store, and still be healthy enough to join the Marines.

I finally discovered what the Emerson squad meant that weekend. Channel 5's version of *Yo! MTV Raps* - a short-lived show called *Pump it Up!* that came on Sunday mornings at 1AM - aired the video "Just to Get a Rep" by Gang Starr. The song had a harder sound than the songs on the group's debut album (*No More Mr. Nice Guy*) and the chorus featured DJ Premier cutting up the Nice-N-Smooth record with surgical precision:

*S-s-s--s--s-s-s, stick up kids is out
to tax! And this is how the story goes…*

"Just to Get a Rep" was the stick-up kid anthem of 1991. About seven months later, I heard the same war call that Emerson chanted when they walked into our gym and busted our asses by 40 points.

Stick up kids is out to tax!

"Yo nigga, that chain is dope. Lemme see that shit."

It was two kids claiming to be members of the Young Guns (aka the YGz), a Mount Vernon street gang voted by *The Daily News* as least likely to accept an invitation to discuss world peace over tea and crumpets. The $14 fake Gucci Link gold chain I had recently purchased from the gift shop on Fourth Avenue in Mount Vernon gave me the look of a baby Slick Rick; the two hooligans mistakenly thought it was real gold. My mother had warned me about visiting friends in the Vernon late at night, and I was now a sitting duck at the train station.

"Stick up kids is out to tax, nigga!" the more rugged-looking of the two shouted again.

Thankfully the chain was a few weeks old at that point, and I had forgotten to put nail polish remover on it (for extra sparkle) before I left the crib earlier that day. When they tried to snatch it, it revealed a green rust ring that it left on my shirt. The green rash caused both of them to explode with hysterical fits of laughter, call me a "broke ass nigga rockin' a fake ass chain" and walk away shaking their heads. That's what I call 'bling around the collar', and that day, a fake piece of jewelry very well may have saved my life.

I can't listen to "Just to Get a Rep" today without instinctively tucking my chain in or preparing to get dunked on. DJ Premier owes me either a $14 Gucci Link or a pair of powder blue Ewing sneakers.

GranD DaDDY IU: "The GirL in the MaLL"

Lefty, the point guard on our team, lent me IU's *Smooth Assassin* CD. I hadn't heard it yet, but he and Fat Calvin kept telling me how dope it was. They weren't bullshitting; it was so dope that I never gave Lefty the CD back. It still sits in my collection today, with his initials written on the jewel case in Sharpie ink. My growing curiosity about sex caused me to zero in on the x-rated tales of one song in particular, "The Girl in the Mall." I didn't know pussy from a microwave oven, but the song lyrics grabbed me by the collar and gave me all types of ideas for the sub-zero day in hell on which I would actually lose my cherry:

30

*I know what you can do, and she
said 'what?'*

*Wrap your lips around this and let
me bust this nut*

*So she agreed to do the deed but
as she grabbed my beef*

*I smacked the SHIT out her, and said
'go brush ya teeth'*

*So she went upstairs, got the Scope
and the Crest*

*When she came back down, the breath
was minty fresh*

*So she dropped to her knees, started
lickin' my knob*

*Then she put it in her mouth and got
on the job*

*And I tell ya right now, the bitch
wasn't perpin'*

*From three blocks away you could hear
the girl slurpin'*

*Then I told her bend over and I stuck
my pole*

Smack dab in the middle of her asshole

IU's graphic sexcapade was the catalyst behind me writing my very first rap. In the spring of '91, I penned "Bronco Billy", an x-rated tale about fuckin', suckin', and other bizarre sexual acts I had never done before (some of them I still haven't tried). I was getting Bs in English class, so it was well-written for my first rap, just not believable. What was believable was moms going ape shit when she found the manuscript sitting on my bed while she was snooping around. I was handled in Florida Evans fashion by moms, had to hear the God damn riot act again, and lost my allowance for two months. Grand Daddy IU owes me $160.

31

social education, hip-hop style

RaP 101

*T*hose "talks" from my folks and grandparents began to intensify and increase in frequency by mid-1991, but I didn't care. I found a way to use my little keyboard with the recorder on it to sample pieces of records and make little bullshit beats with no drums. I would loop up the break beat from Kool & the Gang's "Rated X", slow it way down, and recite "Bronco Billy" to my boys when they came by my crib.

In April of '91, I made Confirmation, to the delight of my grandparents. Whoop-de-doo. After attending Sunday school for two years to make Communion and finally being allowed to consume the bread and wine, it pissed me off when I discovered that they tasted like stir-fried shit. Father Fruitcake (the local church priest) would always rub my shoulders like I was a fly bitch on the sofa or something. After I used my $75 for perfect Sunday school attendance to buy a pair of sneakers and Main Source's *Breaking Atoms* CD, I decided that a black man practicing Catholicism was as logical as a black man voting for David Duke. I haven't entered a church since I made Confirmation except to attend a funeral.

Listening to Paris, Public Enemy, and X-Clan sent me into a black militant upward spiral and inspired me to get special permission to do my book report on *The Autobiography of Malcolm X* as opposed to *Catcher in the Rye*. Arnold Sr. began to grow frustrated with me from what I could tell, but I was straining my brain to fathom why the man who wrote *Dear White Folks* was still praying to a Jesus with a blonde mane. My days of studying the Beatitudes and the periodic table of elements with him were replaced by studying the latest rap tape and getting my initials shaved into the back of my hair.

I dropped out of the school jazz band and little by little began to abandon my bass playing talents, something I regret doing to this day. There was no way I'd find six other brothers my age who were willing to form the next Ohio Players. What I did have was a bunch of records, some writing ability, and a little Chia Pet in the form of a terrible attitude that I was growing.

In late '91, I heard an Ice Cube commercial advertising St. Ides Malt Liquor on the radio. It went something like...

> *All I want for Christmas is my*
> *St. Ides brew*
>
> *And put it in your egg nog.*

I learned the hard way that a 40 oz. of St. Ides won't make your dick hard like the fellas said it would; it'll just make you deathly ill.

One night, the police accused me of robbing a jogger near the Metro-North train station. They slammed my face into a Plexiglass window and pressed a pistol into my back, before making me take off my shirt and stand out in the rain. Those cocksuckers had also accused me of robbing my own apartment right in front of my mother the year before. I hated cops and so did rappers. Going home and turning on Live Squad's song, "Murderaaah", after getting roughed up helped me blow off the steam. I listened intently to them rap about how they "kill muthafuckin' cops with a smile, *King of New York* style."

Rappers fought day in and day out to perpetuate the myth that rap doesn't influence kids; that's a bunch of shit. Whether it was Brand Nubian's pleas for knowledge of self or Eazy-E's senseless ambushing of a hooker, rappers had become the big brothers I never had via their on-record persona. I hung on to every word. My two year rap education crash course was quicker and more intense than my classroom experience in grades K-12 and college combined.

I entered junior high school as a quiet and shy kid. I left as a semi-knucklehead and I knew that one day I'd probably wind up involved in rap in some capacity. I'd eventually stop wearing fake gold chains, calling people faggots for no reason, writing songs about "cookin' pussy on the stove with garlic and cloves" and disrespecting women who could whoop my ass, but shit would never be the same thereafter.

5. SUCKER DJ

*T*he dance floor in the lounge on Milwaukee Avenue in Chicago had a really bizarre flooring pattern. I began to play an imaginary game of *Tetris* with the sections that had been replaced over the years. I didn't clear many rows, but that was the least of my concerns at the moment. It was midnight – I shouldn't have even been able to see the floor.

The warm-up DJ had done his job by getting the party partially pumped with a solid mix of '90s rap. The DJ who took the wheels after him was supposed to set the alley-oop for me; instead, he pulled the fire alarm. I'm not sure which was more of a peeve to me: the fact that he was spinning a party (poorly) using the Ableton software program and had completely unplugged the turntables or the fact that he was there with the rest of us at 2:12 AM, unleashing hazmat levels of halitosis via conversation about retro sneakers and waiting to get paid.

On the other side of the velvet rope, A-list clubs in big cities across the globe book "celebrity" DJs - aka famous entertainers and their siblings who took trips to Guitar Center to pick up Serato "Itch" when their latest Hollywood endeavors tanked - to DJ parties for a four or five digit pay day on the night they lose their DJ cherry. If they suck, it's OK. They're famous entertainers; the DJ thing is at best their new form of income and at worst a novelty for the press to blog about.

As for me, I'm in Chi-Town watching DJ Gingivitis not only being unafraid to suck, but getting paid to suck. Playing a 72 BPM trap-rap song followed by Mobb Deep's "Cop Hell" with 5 seconds of dead air between them is something that may have cost Mr. Gingivitis his life 16 years prior, in 1992. That was the year that it could have cost me mine for sucking half as much.

The Punk behind the Wheels

In the midst of my freshman year at Mamaroneck High School, I went from rap student to rap participant. My port of entry (with the exception of my "Bronco Billy" rhyme and terse looped samples) was the turntables. Not many DJs would be willing to part with a fully functional pair of Gemini belt drive turntables and a mixer for $150, but Chip knew my plight. As my best friend Davian's older brother, Chip knew I couldn't scrape up much more scratch than that with my weekly paper route. He was also tired of me hanging around his crib in Mount Vernon at all hours of the night asking to fuck around on the tables. When he finally let me cop that DJ set-up from him, I was on my road to copy-catting the turntable wizardry of heavyweights of the time like DJ Scratch, DJ Magic Mike, DJ Miz, DJ Vanguard, DJ Aladdin, and DJ Richie Rich. The movie *Juice* had just ended its theatrical run and made everyone my crew go through a phase of wanting to become either a hoodlum or a DJ. While Davian was knuckling kids down and temporarily calling himself Bishop, I was walking around school with jumbo headphones on and flashing back to Omar Epps doing his wack DJ GQ routine and getting props for it in the Mixxmaster Massacre.

My immediate goals were to make a blend last longer than three seconds and get off a zigga-zigga scratch, but I was as heavy handed as the Russian on the night he croaked Apollo Creed in *Rocky IV*. With a paltry month of experience under my belt, my boy Jorge asked me to DJ a small party at his crib.

"C'mon J-Dawg, you know I'll have girls there. Maybe your virgin ass can get some butt, the DJ always gets laid," Jorge half joked and half assured. "Just a small party, like 20 people."

After 30 minutes of "stop being a fag" I agreed to DJ my first party on Saturday, April 11th, 1992. Meanwhile, the belt drive turntables dragged slowly with every heavy handed scratch I attempted while practicing. I mixed funk records with outdated Sleeping Bag Records 12"s, sounding like sneakers in a dryer. I also still had my "High Rollers" 12" with my wet dream fodder on the album jacket, in addition to completely random rap records like Stetsasonic's *In Full Gear*, Maestro Fresh Wes' *Symphony in Effect* and Stezo's *Crazy Noise*. They were all good records, but of zero help at the time.

"Nigga, you play these records, you're getting your doofy ass thrown off the tables," Davian warned me with a bout of laughter. He continued to snap on me as he thumbed through my one specialized crate that had an index card with JORGE PARTY scribbled on it taped to the side. "We gotta go to Fordham Road and get you some shit that's fat."

It almost felt like Duke the Trainer was inside of me, telling me to leave the parties alone until I got better, kind of like how he told Apollo to throw in the towel as he was getting his ass mopped by the Russian. But Rocky never stopped the fight, and neither did Davian or Willie. The three of us hopped (we never paid) the Metro-North train to Fordham Road in the Bronx. I picked up all of the hottest shit that the Music Factory record store had at the time: A Tribe

Called Quest's "Scenario Remix," Das Efx's' "They Want Efx," Pete Rock & CL Smooth's "T.R.O.Y.," a Kenny Dope break beat 12" and Gangstarr's "Take It Personal."

I may as well have played Right Said Fred at a gang truce meeting. I rocked all of my life-saver records back to back at the party and 30 minutes in, all I had left to play was Craig G's "Droppin Science." Oops. The turntables were set up outside on Jorge's backyard porch; after 35 minutes it began to rain. Double oops. Some old school heads had gotten word of the party and arrived as unwanted guests. Triple oops. Meanwhile, the general consensus was that I was the wackest DJ in New York and it wasn't long before half the party felt they could do better. I just stood there like a piss-poor prostitute in the rain while every knucklehead in town took turns emulating Martin Lawrence in *House Party*. I wanted to bury my head in the stream behind Jorge's house and inhale, but I knew I thoroughly deserved the property raping that was going down. It was the law of the day during that era when it came to rap. Whether you were a DJ, an MC, a dancer, a producer, whatever - if you sucked in public, you were cold cuts.

Two months prior, KRS-One had tossed portly peacemaker MC Prince Be from PM Dawn off the stage for being wack. DJs that sucked were robbed for their crates and gear and then punched in the face, simply for sucking and not much else. *Showtime at the Apollo* gave amateurs the business live on TV, crushing aspiring artist's dreams like the Russian's final uppercut to Apollo's dome until eventually the Sandman dragged them off the stage to end the misery of being sautéed in front of a rowdy Uptown crowd. You were forced to think long and hard about the repercussions of sucking and the benefits of paying dues before putting yourself out there. Putting in extra time to master your craft before aiming to make a name for yourself on Twitter seems backwards today, but nobody at that time wanted to have any part of the consequences of sucking, like I was.

In the midst of the commotion, the mob ripped the ground wire out of my right turntable, rendering it useless as a buzzing piece of plastic. Davian intervened to spare me further humiliation.

"Y'all niggas leave that nigga's shit alone, man."

Davian was all of 5'9" and was the spitting image of a teenage Big Daddy Kane. He also had a knuckle game so speedy, you'd be laid out on the asphalt before he even cocked back on you. We were Ernie and Bert opposites, but friends on the premise of respect for us being who we really were and not trying to be anyone else. When everyone in school all of a sudden got gangster after the first Cypress Hill album dropped, I remained the same music-obsessed kid with the Walkman that never came off; I guess Davian respected that. I may have been the only person in town to trust him, but he was the only brother real enough to have my back that night. Davian was an irascible kid with a fair share of enemies, but nobody wanted to get their block knocked off for mouthing off to him. People would hem and haw about him and accuse him of burglarizing their cribs, but never to his face because false teeth are expensive. Therefore, that one quick quip from my main man was all it took to end the party.

As I sat in my bedroom the following Monday with only one working turntable, I decided not to DJ in public for awhile. Awhile turned into five years. That's when I felt I was decent enough to get up and rock again without completely sucking.

An 'E' For Effort

*T*he memory of tanking my first party in my freshman year of high school still sticks with me today (years of owning only one working turntable have contributed to my shitty right hand scratch). The music business now has terminal cancer as far as earning revenue from the sale of music goes, particularly from the hip-hop side. An artist's live show is now absolutely crucial to his success, but many haven't gotten the memo. Since the turn of the century, it's been perfectly acceptable for a rapper to stand in one spot and look at the stage floor while rapping about rapping. Miraculously, I've never seen one piece of produce tossed at the stage.

Big Daddy Kane can still come out and do a split when the rest of the artists his age are getting rubbed down with Tiger Balm and eating fried chicken; that's what allows him to survive. It can only be attributed to him touring during the late '80s, when Ice-T, LL Cool J, and NWA - who had ex-convicts on the stage bench pressing 400 pounds, a sofa on stage to serenade broads, and hydraulic cars on the set, respectively - were competing to be the best and thus, everyone was scared to suck. Even rappers who weren't top notch performers had dancers to help their cause. Once hip-hop dancers fell out of fashion, showmanship pretty much became a no-show.

I marvel at old video clips of Heatwave and Earth, Wind & Fire live in concert. They managed to inject choreography into their performances while playing instruments. James Brown fined and fired his band members for showing up to gigs with unpolished shoes. At times I wish I was all-out booed at a show early in my career, because I would've had no choice but to have become a much better performer than I was. Ultimately, I was active at a time when everyone on the bill got a trophy or ended their set to a silent crowd; the incentive to not suck had to come out of pride, not fear.

As I watched DJ Gingivitis in Chicago wait to be paid for sucking or listened to one DJ at the club APT in NYC bitch at another for running Serato on a PC instead of a Mac - then try to mask his mistakes with that fuckin' airhorn sound instead of playing through them - I wondered if those turkeys had ever been afraid to suck. If you're going to start a Mac vs. PC debate at a DJ gig, then go work for Tekserve and die a week later.

Being a sucker DJ at age 15 benefited me in a couple of ways. It made me afraid to ever completely suck in public again (although I never mastered performing or DJing to the level I should have) and it made me funnel my energy into what I really, truly wanted to do - make beats and produce my own songs for some other DJ to play.

6. A BUGGED OUT DAY AT POWER PLAY

"They don't even make these no more man."
- Large Professor

That's the first direct phrase I ever heard from a musical superhero of mine. In the summer of '92, I managed to scrape up my very first recording studio internship. At the time, an internship was one of the few ways that a zero like me could bust into the music business.

Hip-hop studios in those days could be dangerous and filled to the brim with debauchery. People got jumped, laid, drunk, high, and arrested in those joints, so what better an environment for an impressionable 15-year-old who was already living vicariously through rap music to spend an entire month in?

Reading the liner notes to my favorite rap albums during math class (while my teacher was talking about some shit called the Pythagorean Theorem) had finally paid off. After combing the Queens Yellow Pages at my grandparents' house, I found the number to Power Play Studios in Long Island City, which I had recognized from my academic distractions. One phone call got me a meeting with Carey, one of the studio managers.

"I thought this was a rap studio," was the first thing I said when I saw Carey.

"You're still a baby," he retorted. "You know your shit, but you're still a baby."

Carey looked like he belonged in The Doors, but the fact that he gave me a chance to intern was huge. Not many major recording studios at that time would allow some high school punk into the operation, but my knowledge of records and relative maturity for my age were enough to convince him to reel me in for summer sessions. If nothing else, it kept me occupied when I came back to Queens on weekends and afforded me a chance to see how much shorter rappers are in person.

I threw out trash, bought Twinkies, and Windexed the Ms. Pac Man machine that Akinyele and DJ Rob Swift couldn't stop stuffing quarters into during their breaks in recording the former's *Vagina Diner* album. I cleaned strange concoctions of piss and blunt ashes out of a few toilets and learned to vacuum like a pro. Even Mr. Belvedere couldn't fuck with me. My monetary compensation for the butler act? One time I found 50 cents in the Ms. Pac-Man machine coin return. My real reward was when Carey let me observe Large Professor working on *Vagina Diner* and a few of the sessions for Roxanne Shante's *The Bitch Is Back* album. I was allowed to spend an hour each day in a session.

I don't know what grabbed my attention more, Large rummaging through a beat up box of 45s or Akinyele rapping about a "homemade abortion" for his girlfriend's pregnancy in the song they were working on, "I Luh Huh." Had I still been in the eighth grade, maybe I would've run around school spewing those views on birth control. Fortunately, I was going into the tenth grade and knew a little better. It didn't stop me from playing the song in my Gender Issues class two years later to the disgust of a room full of spoiled brat feminist chicks, though.

The rappers were cool, but my attention kept reverting back to the E-Mu SP-1200 sampling drum machine that Large was wielding like a pro. I had seen one of my idol producers of the moment, Pete Rock, with one in *The Source* magazine earlier that summer. It was mentioned in songs again and again. It also looked easier to use than the Ensoniq EPS-16, the goofy-looking keyboard sampler that the guy showed me at Sam Ash Music store when I went in there saying, "I want to make songs like those 45 King albums." I eventually asked Large the question that earned me that response that I still joke with him about today. His statement was false; E-Mu had just manufactured a short run of SP-1200s. I discovered this when I went to Manny's Music in midtown Manhattan to inquire about alternatives to the EPS-16 at the end of the summer.

Every dime of the $2,000 I earned as a custodian in my old middle school hosing dried spit off the Wall of Phlegm in the boys' locker room the previous two summers went towards purchasing this black and gray box with assorted sliders and buttons. I was elated that I could finally put some real music to "Bronco Billy" (which had since undergone a title change and become "Dr. Dick Down"). I got jittery when I brought the SP home, plugged it in, and grabbed the Kool & the Gang record, ready to loop up the break. But the buzz died when I learned the golden rule when it comes to musical equipment: Never read the instruction manual, just fuck around on the machine until you figure it out. Reading the manual confused me even more and caused me to implode in frustration after three days of barely getting a sound out of the thing. $2,000 was a Powerball win to the average teenager; I had just blown it on a useless drum machine. My initial SP failure was a sign that my other budding hobby of football might be the way to go. I put the SP back in the box along with my hopes of someday becoming the next 45 King, and then I threw it into my closet under a snowsuit that had been in there since "Thriller" hit the charts ten years prior. My Power Play internship ended when I went back to high school in the fall; I was back to square zero.

7. MAN VS. MACHINES

Football was initially just another avenue to get laid. I didn't do much socializing at yuppie and meathead-laden MHS, so sports were my pass. I made numerous pleas and attempts to live with my grandparents and attend Springfield Gardens High School, my zone high school in Queens. When Arnold Sr. (a stickler for academia who shunned the ultra-rowdy Springfield) shut that down, I considered borrowing an address from a friend who lived in Yonkers and attended Charles E. Gorton High School. He was the same friend who played me a hard-ass demo by a group called The Warlox (who later became famous as Jadakiss and The Lox) called "Duck or Get Bucked." They supposedly went to Gorton and had rap under wraps.

"G-High has mad fly Spanish honeys man," he would entice. "Niggas up in there freestylin', the whole shit." I was willing to do almost anything to leave MHS, but my school teacher mother wasn't about to sanction me trading academics for cool rap aesthetics and fly bitches (on top of taking three buses to get to Gorton).

So MHS it was, and although I really didn't give a fuck about football, I got damn good at it. Hanging out with Davian and the fellas did more than get me acclimated with senseless mischief; it improved my speed tenfold. One time Terell told all of us piss in a super-sized McDonald's cup, but he didn't tell us why. Shortly after, he walked into the ajar rear kitchen door of the China Lion restaurant and threw the cup of human lemonade dead in the face of an employee without provocation. I was frozen with shock, but when I saw the five angry chefs on our trail wielding big-ass kitchen knives, I realized for the first time in my life that I had crackhead speed. By the summer of '92, I was benching 230 pounds and running a 4.5 in the 40-yard dash as a 200 pound 15-year-old.

"Stray Dawg, have you ever thought about playing football in college?"

Coach Chaps asked me that three or four times during my JV season. My nickname, J-Dawg (acquired via my well-known fascination with Tim Dog's *Penicillin On Wax* album), graduated to "Stray Dawg" when I laid one of my teammates out with a blindside hit, gave him a mild concussion, and put him out of commission for the season. Chaps even told me that if I kept it up, a potential football scholarship could pop up. Maybe this was my ticket and I was blowing time sitting there unsuccessfully doodling with the SP-1200 before bedtime.

The coaches kept pushing me to pursue a path on the gridiron, but I didn't have the dedication to learn the intricacies of the 4-3 defense while still trying to decode this machine I had just blown all of my bread on. Ultimately, I never had to choose between football and rap. The forces of nature did it for me when I got nailed with a serious injury running track. I eventually wound up in New Rochelle Hospital for a week of spinal traction, jump-starting an arduous eight month recovery process for a pair of herniated disks in my lower back.

One of the few people to visit me during my 168-hour hospital stay was my pops, who bought me Threat's *Sickinnahead* album on cassette to cheer me up. I picked up The Ultramagnetic MCs' *The Four Horsemen* tape the day before I was admitted to the hospital, and day in and out I would lay up in the bed drinking Suncup orange juice and analyzing those two rap albums on my Walkman. I think I chewed up 16 AA bodega batteries that week, while my spine was slowly being expanded like an accordion.

Rumor had it that *The Four Horsemen* was done entirely on an SP-1200. I had gradually begun to get some sounds out of mine before I was admitted to the hospital, and Ultra's spinning sonic typhoon made me want to attempt a junior version. Although technology has since eclipsed its abilities tenfold, the SP is still regarded by the rap elite as the greatest sampling drum machine ever manufactured. Every sound that came out of it had a trademark lo-fi ring and a staggering number of masterfully produced rap albums were crafted with the SP. Unfortunately, it only had 10 seconds of sampling memory split into 2.5 second chunks over four buttons, which was paltry. Most producers at the time who used the SP connected it to another sampler (like an Akai S950) via MIDI cables to give themselves more sampling time and access to filters and special effects. It was rare that anyone used one SP by itself and made complete-sounding beats with it, but I somehow heard that the Ultra albums were exceptions. Whether the hearsay was true or not, I didn't know, but my belief in the rumor inspired me to do everything I could with that machine that didn't involve a soldering iron.

The samples on *The Four Horsemen* were broken up into pieces instead of whole loops. With the memory limitations on the SP, you really had no choice but to splice the music into tiny fragments of sound. Producers were getting taken to the ATM by labels, artists, and publishers for copyright infringement, so Ultra's method of altering samples until they were unrecognizable was also financially astute.

When I popped in the Threat tape, I marveled at how one album could be built almost exclusively on elements of Zapp and P-Funk (samples which had already been run into the pavement by that time), but not sound the least bit stale. Every beat was a densely-packed ride, like a Compton-drive-by-suitable rendition of a Public Enemy production. Listening to the wall of sound on *Sickinnahead* made me realize at an extremely young age that the music you choose to sample is irrelevant; how you arrange and splice what you use is what gives the beat its own identity. Therefore, if you couldn't afford the $100 rare records that Pete Rock was using, you could still make a dope beat out of a trip to the local library. I kept that theory in the back of my head and applied it a decade later when finding ways to make funky beats out of French accordion music and foreign chant songs.

By the time I made it back to civilization, I had a plan - I was going to dump football, dump the entire high school social experience, and somehow be the only kid in America not named Large Professor to master the SP-1200 before he graduated high school.

a Lesson in sampling

If I put down my yellow Sony Sports Walkman and took my headphones off during my last two years of high school, it was only to take a shit. (A lesson I learned when I accidentally dropped my Walkman in one of the toilets at MHS.) I even kept my Aiwa headphones glued to my dome in class. Miraculously, I got by on fumes and maintained a B average in a solid academic school as a constantly plugged in space cadet.

"Niggas be callin' your name and you don't hear shit with them big ass headphones on," joked Jerry, a schoolmate who also made a hobby out of the microphone and the turntables. Jerry and Omar would always shout up to my window from the street like Bishop when he was looking for Q in *Juice*. I was the only kid in town with equipment, so now everyone made demos at my crib after school. I was usually busy decoding the SP, so I'd front on them by pulling my curtain shut and killing the lights to appear like I wasn't home.

"You be in a zone Jay, word, Jay be zoning like a muthafucka," Jerry continued. Everyone in "The Commons" (aka the black, Latino, and hip-hoppy white kid section of MHS) broke out laughing.

Tyrone jumped in, "Jay be spacing the fuck out with that Walkman!"

Someone else sounded off, "Yo J-Dawg, you wear those headphones when you fuckin' a bitch?! Gettin' tips on tape from Long Dong Silver and shit? The nigga Jay be straight zoning!"

The fellas had unintentionally given me the moniker that I still use today.

With a tedious healing process for my back injury lying ahead, I had a lot of spare time. Whenever I wasn't out looking for record collections on the sidewalk waiting for sanitation pick-up, I was discovering that putting samples on cassette tapes, re-sampling them while they were hi-speed dubbing to another tape, and slowing them back down in the SP gave me more sampling memory. A fellow aspiring beat maker from the Bronx once asked me how the fuck I fit two long samples into the SP with only ten seconds of memory. You can discover these types of tricks when you're not getting laid, don't drink or smoke weed, and are ordered by a doctor to remain sedentary all afternoon.

My health prevented me from getting an after school job, so my pockets sounded like Marley Marl tambourines most of the time. Anything I could scrape up went to staying up on all the newest rap albums and keeping my fingers dusty at record conventions in Manhattan. At times, I had to borrow records to sample from Keith, the coach of our neighborhood summer league basketball team in Mamaroneck who doubled as a youth counselor at school. Keith was sort of like a father figure, but I'll always remember him most for allowing me to borrow his records. That was a privilege that nobody else got. It was probably because I was 16 years old in 1993 and knew who Flip Wilson was.

"Yo Dawg, I can't dig all that rappity rap," he would tease, while sitting in his office with a fisherman bucket hat on and his natural sticking out the sides. "All that scratchin' is makin' me itch brother, but you go ahead and do your thing. Just make sure you don't scratch up my shit."

I created about 30-40 songs in my bedroom, but I recorded them on the same Gemini mixer Chip had given me a year and a half ago. They sounded like shit; I needed to book some studio time. Yeah, studio time: the expensive toll plaza that served as a barrier between the serious and the hobbyists on the other side of the water. At a time when Pro Tools was probably a name for some little known hardware kit, studio time was the only option to make your ideas a sonic reality unless you could afford and store $50,000 worth of equipment. Money was scarce, but I knew I had some shit worth the studio time after an intensive year of honing my craft.

Arnold Sr. wasn't thrilled with me pursuing this rap thing. Rev. Calvin Butts and C. Delores Tucker were making noise by literally smashing explicit rap cassettes in the streets on the news. Rap had recently garnered much more controversy and negative media buzz with the release of Dr. Dre's *The Chronic* and Snoop Doggy Dogg's *Doggystyle* albums. The fact that Snoop was trying to beat a murder rap didn't help rap's rap. I kicked a rhyme for Arnold Sr. one day while sitting in the living room, upon his request. He was a harder judge than Simon Cowell. At the sound of the very first "fuck" out of my mouth, he cut me off and told me to go back to playing bass guitar.

My grandmother threw me a life preserver when she forked over $60 for two hours of studio time at Clockwork Studios on Mamaroneck Ave., a small joint I discovered when I left Jerry's crib one day. I needed to record three songs in one hour; mistakes literally cost money back then. I couldn't afford a two inch reel to reel tape either (they were upwards of $150 at the time), so that little finance-tinged mathematics problem meant I had to be a one take Jake on the microphone. The engineer recorded me rapping and the SP playing my pre-arranged beat at the same time, right directly to a tape cassette. If I fucked up, we had to start all over again and the clock of Clockwork was running. In the weeks leading up to the sessions, I rehearsed my lines like I was preparing for a date with Jasmine Guy and the right delivery would get the drawers down. Being prepared for an hour of studio time was the difference between a one song demo and an EP. I would take the final tape home and overdub the scratches using two tape decks.

Recording studios are nearly obsolete in 2011, as affordable do-it-yourself technology has kicked them in the ass and made things easier. In 1993 though, working in a studio or scraping up funds to buy time in one was standard protocol. Their costly fees separated those who just rapped in the lunchroom from those who were really trying to jam a foot in the door. The exorbitant cost of studio time didn't allow much room for anything short of perfection or quality-sounding mistakes.

With current software programs possessing the ability to do everything short of making the beat for you and performing your vocals on command, technological advancements have ushered in laziness from musicians. I realized this when I saw a software program that contained 24 different vinyl static sounds. Getting a crate of deep fried 45s and finding 24 different static sounds yourself is the essence of production, or so I thought. As far as vocals go, the concept of "punching-in" (recording rap vocal tracks piece by piece, as opposed to nailing a whole stanza in one take) has also reinforced laziness, as well as poor breath control from rappers. When it's time to perform live, you have to recite songs from top to bottom with no chance to catch your breath or tell the engineer to stop recording. I've always felt that limitations spark creativity and enhance skill. The essence of hip-hop is to make something out of nothing. I picked up that tidbit in the eleventh grade and I was on my way.

My back injury eventually healed itself to where the actual pain was gone, but by then, I wasn't even watching *Monday Night Football* anymore. The injury was somewhat of a blessing; it forced me down the path I needed to be trudging. I was now a 16-year-old musicologist and SP-1200 wizard with some funky shit, I just had to get it to the "Wright" man.

On the SP-1200
(Mid-'90s)

8. CHAIRMAN OF THE BOARD

"man hurry up, these niggas are looking at me like i'm a detective."

My pops was a little nervous. We had just come from Whitestone Cinemas in the Bronx, where we saw *The Program*, a college football movie starring Omar Epps and Halle Berry. A character in the movie suffered a career-ending injury, forcing him to give up his NFL goal. He was without education, which relegated him to the dirt poor Deep South and a career doing something that teachers warn us we'll wind up doing if we fuck up in school. My injury meant football was over for me too, and I chose an even more stable career to pursue at age 16 - the music business. It offers cool little perks like lawsuits, bankruptcy, and tax trouble, but my parents miraculously supported the move as long as my grades stayed decent. My six hours a day on the SP-1200, two hours a day writing, and weekly record-hunting missions over the last year served as the necessary requisites for an entry pass into this unstable business.

After the movie, pops drove me over to 80 Horton Avenue in New Rochelle. The building was adjacent to "The Jets" (aka The Robert Hartley Housing Projects), the roughest projects in New Rochelle. It was also the home of the master - DJ Vance Wright, aka Slick Rick's DJ and producer.

At the time, Vance was one of the few brothers in Westchester County really making any noise. Pete Rock had blown the fuck up and really put Mount Vernon on the map in the previous two years, but Vance had a recording studio; that's where I needed to be.

For the past year, I had been trying to get to Vance through some of my people at MHS, who happened to be his cousins. Vance was a busy man though, and harder to find than a copy of Bob James' "Mardi Gras" breakbeat with no bells in it. After finally setting up a meeting, there I was, standing in the hallway holding my demo tape. Meanwhile, pops was outside in what looked like an unmarked cop car near the corner of Horton and Brook, the most thorough corner in New Ro.

Knock, knock...no answer.

"Vance stood me up, he's playin' me," I said to myself. I figured all of Horton and Brook had the car surrounded by now, so I descended the stairs and went back home to pursue plan B, which was polishing my craft and not worrying about "getting on."

"YO my nigga, I almost got my fuckin' head taken off, but I got you a meeting with Vance for real. He's got a new studio called Vee-Dubbs."

It was Kevin Severe, my best friend and rap partner. Kev was and still is the brother I never had; all we did was sit around analyze music all day. Even broads and socializing took a backseat to whatever new shit was out. His little brother would steal tapes from the now defunct New Rochelle mall every week, and we'd chill in the Mamaroneck train station and listen to 'em while Kev engaged in his weekend job folding newspapers.

It was now March of 1994, four months after Vance stood me up and left me standing in the hallway of 80 Horton. Apparently Kev was turning the corner of Main and Cliff streets and unknowingly waltzed into Vance's new recording studio unannounced. Living near "The Jets" must've put Vance on edge, because he was ready to put a hot one in Kev's loud ass. Kev pleaded peace in time, and convinced DJ Vance to give me a chance.

On March 24, 1994, I made what I consider my official entry into the music business when I cut out of school with Kev to go finally meet Vance and play him my latest demo. He nodded his head the whole time, but he saw the most potential in my passion for my craft, which prompted him to make me his first intern. Within a week, I was a 17-year-old gofer running errands to get grilled turkey sandwiches for Greg Nice (of Nice-N-Smooth) and listening to stories about he and Smooth B learning of Sleeping Bag Records going out of business by simply going to the office and seeing the gate pulled down. CL Smooth had just finished recording *The Main Ingredient* album with Pete Rock, but he was looking to do outside projects and had opened up a car wash across the street from the studio. An R&B cat that booked sessions got busted by two broads at once, and what transpired afterward showed me that love singers are far more ruthless than rappers can ever be. Ike Turner didn't make gangsta rap. Slick Rick would call the studio from jail, but I never met him. Rappers with current hit videos on BET would pass through the studio to see Vance, and I'd double take like a young green teenager is supposed to.

"You smoke weed Jay?" Vance asked me on one of those rare occasions when we were alone and I was trying not to nerd out and bombard him with a million questions about Greyson & Jasun and Slick Rick albums.

"Nah man, I never tried it," I answered, half embarrassed and half excited. "I need to, though!"

"Get the fuck outta here!" he yelled. Vance spoke in a recliner chair-style conversational tone 99.9 percent of the time, so the volume jump made my heartbeat flutter. "I ever catch you smoking that shit, your ass is outta here. That goes for drinking 40s and smoking cigarettes too." Those were the rules - I was still a minor. Vance spoke to me about vices like an NBA veteran talks to a junior high school point guard prodigy about getting straight As. "Half of this business is fried from smoking and drinking," he continued. "You don't have any bad habits, don't start. Just keep fuckin' with that SP-1200; you'll be the man one day. You do need to get a girlfriend, though."

By the start of my senior year of high school in September, Vance had promoted me to fully paid recording engineer. He gave me most of the studio sessions after 4PM. I was pulling in more money as a 17-year-old than I was at certain points in my professional career. Every solitary dime I made went to records. More specifically, I frequented Venus Records on St. Marks Place and the New York City Record Convention at the Roosevelt Hotel, where my father would drive me on Sunday mornings to blow my weekend earnings on obscure vinyl like a gambling husband at Belmont Racetrack.

I'm almost positive I went to high school my senior year. At least I think I did. My brain was in the studio 24/7. Maybe three people in the halls of MHS knew that I was digging my way into the music biz when I cut out of class at 2:00, and some of the patrons at Vee-Dubbs seemed to forget I was still a kid. One time I was between sessions and decided to get scholarly in the studio lounge by doing homework for Mrs. G's writing class. It was a bit hard to focus with the ambient rap star talk from some cats I'd never seen at the studio before and never saw again. I heard about some big booty chick getting boned, but I didn't hear about any involvement of condoms. I think instead of answering question #12 on my homework with "subject and predicate," I answered with "some bitch is pregnant."

Had my folks known about some of the shit that went down at Vee-Dubbs, my ass would've been a bedroom producer again. At times, I stayed out to 1AM on school nights and 5AM on weekends. But I wouldn't trade those nights for shit.

I did a recording session with Stud Dougie (Grand Puba's DJ) instead of going to my prom. There was no getting head in the back of a limo, just the daily six mile round trip walk from my apartment to the studio and back. When the time came to get my diploma, I walked onstage with my headphones on and ice grilled the school principal (who had to have owned slaves at one point). Within two hours, I was back at Vee-Dubbs like nothing had happened all day.

I finally lost my vinyl cherry with my first production credit for "Fool I Got Your Back", a song I produced for Nice-N-Smooth affiliate Preacher Earl at the studio. I was on wax with the best imitation Pete Rock beat I had in my stash; in my young mind, I had arrived.

A host of Vee-Dubbs characters gave me an early glimpse of the music business, but a few stood out amongst the rest.

The YGz aka the Young Guns

*T*he YGz were a giant group of weapon-wielding, excessive-number-of-push-up-doing gentlemen that you wouldn't want to be caught humming the theme song to *Gilligan's Island* around. Hailing from Mount Vernon, they had affiliations with Pete Rock, Eddie F, and of course, Vance. Their *Street Nigga* EP had a few local hits on it, but when it came to doling out drubbings, they went platinum enough times to make it to the 10 o'clock news. After their young recruits caught me slipping with the fake Gucci Link at the train station in '91, I vowed to do my best to never cross paths with a YG again. No dice.

Vance made a trip to Cross County Mall in Yonkers on the fall 1995 evening that the main MCs in the group (Kenny and Tommy) were coming to the studio to do edits to "Groove On", a Pete-Rock produced 12" they were preparing to release.

"I'll be back at 10, Kenny and them will be here at 8," Vance said. "You'll be alright. Oh, by the way, they're using the two inch, not the ADAT."

Perfect. I had used the two inch reel to reel machine maybe twice in the 18 months I had been there thus far. I knew it as well as I knew Microeconomics, which I was in the midst of flunking in my first semester in college. The ADAT was the studio standard. It was 7:17 PM, and I had a good hour before I fucked up the YGz two inch reels and got murdered for the ever-maligned engineer mistake. I could see it now, the b-side to the single would be "Faggot Ass Engineer", an autobiographical account of them making a sprinkler system out of my ass and leaving me leaking on the 24-track mixing console.

I prayed. Then portions of a verse from the YGz most well-known song, "Street Nigga", randomly popped into my head:

Straight uptown, from Money Earnin'
Mount V

I carry my tech-9 and troop with the YGz
So when beef comes, I'm ready for war

Put a slug in a nigga and I settle
the score

Like a tic for a tac, my gat bust
the most caps

Kill a muthafucka leave him dead with
the alley cats

Wanna be brave? Dig a grave nigga, that's
where you're going faggot

Bodies being smothered with maggots

Punk niggas shouldn't act tough, don't
even flex rough

I'll beat you til you're black as
a Cocoa Puff

Gotta survive playin' the street game

Splattering fuckin' brains and sellin'
some cocaine

"God, it's me. I know I haven't been to church in about four-and-a-half years," I said softly, while praying up to the drop ceiling and calibrating the two inch reel to reel machine. "Please let this session go smooth until Vance gets back, and don't let me mess up the YGz reels. Please."

Street Niggaz are punctual. Kenny and Tommy showed up at 8PM on the nose, with about 12 other Street Niggaz in tow. They barely fit in the studio. Talk was minimal.

"Where's Vance?" asked Kenny.

"Cc-cross, cross, um, Cross County man, Cross County," I fumbled.

"Word, you the engineer right? Let's get this shit rolling. Here's the reel."

I nervously threaded the tape machine with the reel, praying about as hard as OJ Simpson was at the time to beat his case. A thought then occurred to me:

Maybe if I get on their good side, I'll be safe.

"Man, not for nothing, but that *Street Nigga* EP was the best shit to come out last year!" I blurted suddenly. Yeah, it was an exaggeration, but I really thought *Street Nigga* was a dope record and still do. Why not let it be known when my life was potentially on the line?

"Word! That's what the fuck I mean!" screamed Kenny, giving me a painful pound and becoming thoroughly excited at my potentially life-preserving compliment. "Good lookin'."

I continued to pour on praise through a cloud of second-hand Buddha smoke thick enough to cure glaucoma. Needless to say, I loosened up like a good bowel movement and for three hours, I was safe as a good studio engineer for the YGz.

Greg Nice

Besides being the most animated guest star and humorously nonsensical MC in hip-hop, Greg Nice is a culinary wizard. I never would've thought of making a grilled turkey and cheese sandwich with the turkey and cheese grilled separately.

"You need to grill it separately, that makes it less of a mess," he explained with Wolfgang Puck enthusiasm. After schlepping my gofer self over to the Thru-Way Diner up the street to get his sandwich for the fourth or fifth time, he finally began to open up and tell me stories like the Sleeping Bag Records fiasco. Then he would go on to explain why The Bomb Squad were the greatest hip-hop producers of all time, a sentiment that I agree with to this day. I still bump into Greg from time to time, and surprisingly, he still remembers his old gofer.

BiLLY LOOSE SCreWS aka BiLL BLaSS

Folks in Westchester (more specifically Yonkers) usually remember Billy Loose Screws as Bill Blass, DMX's nemesis in the early 1990s. By the time he began to lock out eight hour sessions on Friday evenings in April of 1995, he was Billy Loose Screws, and his rapping style was as off the wall as his name suggests. He ran with a crew that hailed from the Getty Square and Locust Hill areas of Yonkers, places you just didn't fuck around. But when Billy left the vocal booth, he was the most positive, amicable, and polite artist I ever had the chance to work with in my 15 years in the music business. We recorded upwards of 30 songs, none of which saw the light of day.

Billy was the complete package as an artist, but as I would learn a decade later, the battery of the music business is charged by timing and who you know. I would eventually work with Billy and the rest of the crew outside of the studio, taking two and three buses to Yonkers to do everything from make songs to work on bootleg sample collections to sell in record stores like Music Factory and Rock & Soul.

Walking though the Mulford Gardens Housing Projects (which have since been razed by the city of Yonkers) at night to get music done was enough to scare you into pissing down your leg, but in those days, brushes with danger, violence, and humiliation were merely rites of passage to get into this shit. It's almost like hip-hop was some clandestine after-school program that the participants themselves controlled, and Billy provided some of my finest and earliest memories of what I feel the spirit of making records should be about.

Midnight

Midnight scared the shit out of me when I first met him. He cut hair at Mackadocious barber shop on North Ave. in New Rochelle, and would book studio time at 3AM on Saturday mornings, right after Billy left. He didn't seem too fond of people and walked around with a ferocious dog named Killred, an easy stunt double for the dog that M.O.P used in the "Rugged Neva Smoove" video. Midnight was a one man YGz, but most dudes like that will respect those who act themselves, and Midnight was probably the realest person I've ever worked with in any capacity.

"Man, I don't give a fuck what you sample, just filter out all the highs and make the drums hard," he would order. "Let it distort, I don't give a fuck about the mix." He sounded evil, pissed off, and he never asked for any radio edits. He knew what he was doing wouldn't make a dime and seemingly made music strictly for his own fulfillment. One day, he actually asked me for my opinion on a song he'd just completed.

"Yo man, it's hard," I admitted, not giving up the full truth.

"I know that muthafucka, my shit is always hard," he spat back. "I mean is it good, do you like it?"

"It's...it's," I sputtered.

"Don't bullshit me," he interjected. "If you think the shit is wack, say the shit is wack. I'll respect you more."

I was scared to front on him, and Killred being perched in the corner of the vocal booth in his finest "what nigga?!" pose didn't exactly have a calming effect. But when I stopped bullshitting, he loosened up. As I got older and entered the music biz on a higher scale, I learned to greatly appreciate the rare trait of straightforwardness; Midnight had a whole shitload of that rare trait to spare.

y9'2: Street nigga eP

the first j-zone production (1995)

In my three years at Vee-Dubbs, I crossed paths and worked with countless others I was an young awestruck fan of: Greyson & Jasun, Brand Nubian, Grand Puba, Amil (when she was rapping about sticking bitches up, long before she worked with Jay-Z), and numerous other local acts. But some of the artists we were working with day in and out were either getting locked up or straight quitting. Meanwhile, I discovered a new world while staying up late on Thursday nights because I had no Friday classes at Purchase College - Stretch & Bobbito's Radio Show on 89.9 WKCR-FM. I tried to turn some of the rappers at the studio on to the independent rap method.

"Man these Arsonist, Company Flow, Natural Elements, Juggaknots cats, they're pressing their own vinyl," I would explain. "They're pushing major units of 12" singles; going overseas; making money! No video, no daytime radio, no major label, no shit. We need to do the shit ourselves!" My pleas fell on deaf ears. A lot of the acts that came through the studio still had the 1990 "we gotta get signed" mentality, but we continued churning out demos for another few months. Eventually, I was forced down another avenue when Vance made an announcement.

"I'm closing up Jay, time to keep it moving," said Vance, who had just become a father. "Its time for me to focus on being a father, I gotta fall back with this studio thing." Vance and I would remain lifelong friends, but I would go on to live on campus at Purchase, switch my major to music, and run their 16-track studio. In my downtime, I was trying to follow out my plans of guerilla bum rush, independent, out-the-trunk hustling. I never made a J-Zone solo record until I was two years removed from Vee-Dubbs, but that studio on the corner of Main and Cliff was where I learned to be a man of my word and formulated my plan of attack for the music business.

9. MUSIC FOR *TU MADRE*:
A LESSON IN SELF-PRESERVATION

Arnold Sr. passed away right before Vance shut down shop. I didn't have the balls to see him more than once while he was spending his last days in a hospital in Far Rockaway, Queens. My widowed grandmother was alone, so I permanently moved back home to keep an eye on her.

Whenever I wasn't doing grandson duty, I was making the initial steps in creating my first album, *Music for Tu Madre*. My debut release began as little more than my senior project for the Purchase College music department and a distraction from everything else going on in my life. I produced the entire thing on my own, earning myself the credit I needed to graduate, but I only put my vocals on it because I had a deadline and couldn't find anyone else to rap. Although I had writing potential, my delivery sucked. I eventually got some rap help from two cats I was working with at the time - Al-Shid and Huggy.

Upon the album's completion in December of 1998, I sold cassette tapes of it on my shifts working in the campus game room for pocket change. Disc Makers (the cassette manufacturer I used) refused to duplicate my album because of the plethora of uncleared samples on it, so I ordered blank gold colored cassette shells customized to the length of the album and put the music on them myself from the CD master.

Requests began to pick up around campus from people I didn't even know. At that point, I had to borrow friends' dual cassette decks so I could run them in unison with mine and have multiple *Music For Tu Madre* tapes high-speed dubbing simultaneously. Those who wanted CD-R copies of the album had to wait a week so I could get into the school studio to burn copies in real time from the DAT machine.

The album title was based on a funny Polaroid picture I had taken of my grandmother smoking a blunt, holding a Louisville Slugger, and flipping the camera the bird. With the effects of my grandfather's passing two months after the two celebrated their 50th wedding anniversary still lingering, I tried to do goofball shit like that with my grandmother to pull her out of her funk. The photo eventually became the album cover and I would schlep over to Kinko's Copy Center at all hours of the night to make double-sided color copies for the cassettes.

Within weeks, Purchase outsiders had gotten tape dubs of *Music for Tu Madre* from friends who went home for the weekends. E-mail was a new phenomenon, so folks from all over began contacting me about where, when, and how they could buy my little slapdash album for $10. I had a cool little operation going, but gold tapes and CD-R burns could only take me so far.

"If you press 1000 vinyl copies, I guarantee you you'll sell out of them," Rob C., a British cat from Sound Library Records in the East Village, told me in early 1999. "I'll take 100 copies right now and buy 50 to sell to Mr. Bongos Records back home [in London]."

I priced the manufacturing cost for 1000 pieces of vinyl at Freeze Records on 26th Street in Manhattan and my quote was $1,800. That was 75 percent of what I was worth in life savings.

"Fuck all that, I'm getting an apartment when I graduate," I told Rob. He wasn't about to convince me to go broke for some album that I wasn't even completely sold on my damn self.

I analyzed *Music For Tu Madre* closely while granny-driving back to Queens in a snowstorm one night. I didn't think it was worth an $1800 risk. The production and concepts were kind of like sophomoric nods to KMD's *Mr. Hood* and De La Soul's *3 Feet High and Rising* albums, but putting myself out there as a rapper was a step in the wrong direction as far as I was concerned.

"Just press the damn thing already," Rob would badger every time I went into the Sound Library to dig through their dollar bins.

By February of 1999, my reservations lost to his convincing. I semi-reluctantly spent 3/4 of my life savings to press *Music for Tu Madre* on vinyl. My final decision came down to looking at the album as an expensive resume for my production. I didn't have enough of a name to sell my beats at the time, so I'd have to get them heard through my own projects. Pete Rock, Dr. Dre, and DJ Premier all became known via producing for their own groups first; putting the shit out was the only option. The photo of my grandmother inspired the name Old Maid Entertainment for this overnight label of mine, and I was now an aspiring hip-hop producer who was slowly becoming an artist and a trial-by-fire CEO by accident.

Getting your shit played on Stretch & Bobbito's radio show was like a minor league equivalent of DJ Funkmaster Flex dropping a bomb on your song on Hot 97. After being a fan of the show for years, my man DJ Eli from Purchase passed Bobbito a copy of my album and he was running it on a weekly basis. It was only a matter of time before Bob booked me to perform my first show at the Nuyorican Poets Café in the East Village, the night before my college graduation. That "I ain't never stepping on stage" shit took a bullet when I realized that doing so was the only way to promote my music and get rid of the boxes of vinyl piled up in my college dorm. To my surprise, doing shows wasn't all that nerve-racking.

My first crew was assembled in the same spur-of-the-moment fashion as my album's creation and release; Huggy, Shid, and my radio show partner from college, Dick $tallion, became the Old Maid Billionaires.

Little by little, distributors, magazines, record store employees (one of whom, a young kid from Michigan named DJ Contakt, eventually moved to Queens and became my DJ), and even casual fans began to call about my accidental debut album. I was one of very few artists on NYC's late '90s independent rap scene to come out with a full-length album out of nowhere and it was ass backwards. With no 12" single for radio, no-promotion, and no established artists co-signing me, putting out a record in that fashion in 1999 meant one of two things - I was either a trendsetter who had a major set of balls or I really had no fuckin' clue of how the music business worked. I would say it was more a case of the latter, but that naivety and ignorance are what made the whole experience so damn fun.

I slid copies of my album into mailings I did while interning at Relativity Records during my last semester of college. DJs were undoubtedly perplexed when they got a package with gangster-ass Dayton Family and Shoestring records, but there was a copy of J-Zone's *Music for Tu Madre* randomly thrown in. Fat Beats record store was selling a box of 30 records per week and internet sites specializing in independent rap releases like Sandbox (in NYC) and Hiphopsite (in Las Vegas) began to inquire about the album. Early 1999 was the tail end of an era when you could release independent music without bells and whistles and still stand a chance of being noticed. As one of about 30 indie rap records on the wall at Fat Beats, it was only a matter of time before someone saw the Polaroid of my grandmother living the thug life on the cover and asked a store clerk to play my shit. By 2002, the indie rap market had become so flooded with arbitrary releases that you needed Don King, Berry Gordy, Jerry Maguire, and Russell Simmons to get some recognition.

I had to cut class frequently during my last semester of school to drive to Manhattan for deliveries. Sandbox decided to carry the cassette tape, so that meant mastering the art of lane-changing on the Major Deegan Expressway while simultaneously cutting out the artwork with the orange-handled scissors I kept in my glove compartment. One time, I forgot to tell my grandmother a vinyl shipment was coming to the house when I was away at school.

"What in the hell are all these damn boxes coming here for you from UPS!?" she screamed at me over the phone. She was pissed off enough to call my apartment at school to berate me.

"They're albums Grandma," I explained. "I'll pick them up when I come home this weekend."

"Shit!" she spewed in her trademark nastiness. "I don't give a damn if you're in Hong Kong nigger, you bring me some duck sauce and then get this shit out of my living room!"

The week after graduation, I went down to the Queens county courthouse on Sutphin Boulevard and made Old Maid Entertainment an official business (and eventually, a corporation). After pressing second and third runs of *Music for Tu Madre*, the remaining money went toward building my own recording studio (which I dubbed "Pimp Palace East") in my basement. Every aspect of the Old Maid approach was low budget and D.I.Y., but even when help came along, it didn't appeal to me. Record deals came in from small independent labels, but if I made it to record store shelves with zero help, I didn't need anyone else taking my money. To sell 4,000 copies of an out-of-nowhere, bar code-less album in three months wasn't too shabby. I was able to quit my short-lived, post-college graduation job at The Automobile Club of America (AAA) as a call dispatcher soon after.

"Why do you have all those records in the trunk of your car?" asked my airhead co-worker, who curiously peered over my shoulder during our coffee break in the parking lot. "Nobody plays records anymore." I divulged to her the details of my obscure musical operation.

"That's cool," she said, with a partial understanding of what I was talking about. "So if you're a musician, why are you working in this place?"

I gave AAA my two weeks notice and officially became a full-time musician. Sometimes airheads know a thing or two about success; *Jersey Shore* was a big time hit, you know.

In the midst of my new found excitement, Herbie succumbed to pancreatic cancer. I didn't yet fully appreciate his views on betrayal and unrequited decency though, with the cloud I was on. As a green 22-year-old, I hilariously expected the best out of people and believed that nice guys really finished first. Fans of my music often ask why I went from innocently poking fun at commercial rap music with an aura of extreme humility on *Music for Tu Madre*, to arrogantly lambasting everybody in my path in the years to come. It's called getting introduced to the real world. Within a year, I purposely made the transition from humble newcomer to the crass, foul-mouthed black sheep of the independent hip-hop scene. In short, the next time J-Zone and the Old Maid Billionaires performed at the Nuyorican Poets Café, we pissed off a bunch of head wrap-wearing strippers moonlighting as ethereal slam poets and got tossed out of the venue mid-way through our set.

Sometimes I adhered to that *Music for Tu Madre* D.I.Y. mentality down the line and sometimes I didn't, but for better or worse, the "go for self" modus operandi had become permanently encoded in my DNA. Growing up, I always had a tremendous amount of respect for Mob Style, a Harlem-based rap group from the early '90s. Lead rapper AZ (who I would eventually have the pleasure of meeting and interviewing for a magazine) would often finance and manufacture projects himself, bypassing record labels and other music business vultures in a self-run operation on par with regional rap artists in the south and on the west coast. AZ's approach was all the more ground-breaking considering that circa 1990, just about everyone in New York putting out music had a major record deal. When labels like Def Jam, Atlantic, and Mercury didn't give the Mob Styles, E-40s, and Master Ps of the world a chance, they found alternatives. Big budgets, worldwide recognition, and major promotion were sidestepped for total creative and financial control, niche audiences, and a low budget aesthetic that made exaggerated murder scene album covers and monaural mix downs strangely appealing.

What budget? early master p + az tapes

The 100 percent D.I.Y days of *Music for Tu Madre* were my most exciting and oblivious ones in the music biz. Each day brought a new lesson or experience. A little more recognition and money were soon to follow, but the excitement eventually hit a plateau and fizzled out like Sho'Nuff's glow in the final fight against Bruce Leroy. The migraines that came with my moves up the music biz ladder sometimes made me wish I had kept my job at AAA and went back to sloppily cutting cassette artwork with scissors in traffic for a modest-paying hobby.

10. LEGAL ACTION FROM A PIMP

I never cower from the fact that I'm a 90 percent sample-based producer. Creative copyright infringement makes my dick hard. From the moment EPMD's "You Gots to Chill" came on *Yo! MTV Raps* that afternoon in 1989, sampling has been the bait that has hooked me to hip-hop. Vinyl, cassettes, my endless collection of VHS tapes that have been stuffed to the lead out strips with old TV shows, infomercials, and obscure movies - they all inspired my entire aesthetic and got thoroughly raided when I was putting my trademark wall of sound style together. There's nothing like watching an episode *of Bewitched!* and hearing Dick York say something in his nerdy voice, then flipping his phrase out of context into something x-rated or weaving it into a rap song about whoopin' somebody's ass. Sampling allows that type of contrast, and contrary to criticism, it takes a hell of an ear to hear Mr. Wilson say something on *Dennis the Menace* and imagine it dead smack in the middle of a rap song about blow jobs.

In the '90s, artists got jack-hammered with legal action for copyright infringement to no end, even those not on major labels. Everyone was petro; someone could really piss on your picnic retroactively if you made some money.

Technically, anything you pilfer without permission can land your ass in hot water if you're caught, regardless of your level of success. Gilbert O'Sullivan took Biz Markie to trial for an uncleared sample circa 1991, forever changing the art form of sampling. Artists and producers had their records snatched off shelves and their royalties recouped for decades because a publisher or an ex-artist turned crack head got desperate. The artists, publishers, and labels that own the rights to the sources that we sample throw all types of cockamamie charges into infringement lawsuits - religious reasons, disagreement with the lyrical content that we put over the samples - and it's all a bunch of shit. For the right price, nine out of ten muthafuckas will back off, but if you wondered why that incredible Ghostface Killah song that leaked on the internet didn't make his album or why a release was delayed for an extra five months, blame the costly and headache-inducing process of sample clearance.

That artistic barricade never stopped me from sampling. I never gave a shit. Why? There was one unwritten rule that turned sampling from an egregious and costly taboo into a calculated business risk in the eyes of many - if they can't catch it, they can't catch you. Here are the ways you can go about not getting your ass taken to Judge Wapner for samples:

1. Get permission and clear 'em.
2. Alter 'em beyond recognition to the average ear.
3. Have paltry record sales and make sofa change money. You'll soar below the radar of lawyers, snitches, musicologists, and the washed up artist you sampled. Pinning legal action on someone who isn't making much money is a waste of time and funds.
4. Sample shit that's so obscure, that the likelihood of anyone identifying it is equal to being black, broke, and meeting your dream girl in New York City.

Options 2-4 applied to me, so I always felt it was worth the risk. One time in particular, I felt wrong. When I got the e-mail on the night DJ Jam Master Jay was murdered, my mood was already in the toilet.

"You gotta be shittin' me!" I screamed loud enough to awaken my slurring, denture-less grandmother. I was being threatened with a lawsuit from Rudy Ray Moore (aka Dolemite), the pimped-out and x-rated comedian that I had admired since I found his record in my pops' collection in 1990. His manager wanted roughly 25 percent of my total income for the year of 2002 in damages for an uncleared sample that I used on my album, *Pimps Don't Pay Taxes*. Apparently, someone wrote an online review of the album and noted the sample; a quick internet search of Mr. Moore's name by his manager was enough to catch me by the ankles.

I was shocked, petrified, flattered, and saddened when I opened that e-mail. The shock came from me realizing that my obscurity outside of indie rap circles wasn't so extreme that I couldn't get nailed. The fear was that these folks would wipe me out completely for the fuck of it. I was flattered that I had made it that far onto the radar for anyone to care. The sadness came from being threatened with legal action by someone I had idolized for more than half of my life. It's like being a Michael Jordan fan, then he sues you because you used one of his moves without permission and said, "You better eat your Wheaties" afterward, then uploaded it to YouTube. I couldn't be mad though; sampling is technically illegal and I knew it.

After settling out of court, you'd probably assume I stopped sampling.

caught! can i get a witness?

Fuck that. I just adhered to rules 2-4 harder than ever before and did my best to take the art of the sample flip and the tedious process of sample searching to levels never done before. I did attempt the first rule once, when I produced "Santana DVX" (featuring E-40) for the Lonely Island, a rapping trio of comedic geniuses from *Saturday Night Live*. Due to the fact that Lonely Island were on Universal Records and featured Justin Timberlake, T-Pain, and a host of other artists that were far more notable than I on their album, Universal threw away the dice and cleared all samples. The process delayed the shit out of everything. After forking up a hefty sum of upfront money and surrendering my entire share of the publishing to the guy I sampled, I understood why artists on major labels used crappy keyboard beats with no samples for so long. I don't give a fuck though, I'll still sample your shit and you won't be able to tell.

Mr. Rudy Ray Moore passed away in 2008, and all jokes on my being busted aside, the black comedy world lost an icon when he left this Earth. I just hope that some of my money went to my hero and not to the legal eagles that don't respect sampling as a legitimate and creative approach to making music.

11. DON'T HOLLA! NO, NEVER, GOODBYE

"I JUST GAVE A MUTHAFUCKA A POUND, A COMPLIMENT, TOLD HIM MY NAME AND I WAS OUT. PEACE." - GURU (RIP)

If you were to scrape up every particle of sincerity in the music business and feed it to a roach, he'd still have enough room in his system to repeat the feeding process 17 more times before he was full. It's also worth noting that the music biz is one of the only universes in which showing up late and not keeping your word will not only *not* get you killed or fired, but will in some cases increase your stock. Musicians who show up to gigs two hours late are stoned and drunken geniuses. Managers face deep in their iPhones talking faster than the Micro Machine man all of a sudden have relevance after most likely being slapped around throughout adolescence.

It's obvious that in the colossal world of pop stars, blowing smoke up someone's ass is protocol. But I had to learn the hard way that even in the cellar of the underground music scene, the same set of principles lurk. Simply put, the indie rap scene of the early 2000s was a poor man's mainstream. You may have had a better chance making it there than signing with Def Jam, but you'd be up against a similar set of disturbances.

It takes a certain type of parasite to fit right in as a part of the entertainment puzzle - a place where men of their word long to hear the words no, never, and goodbye like they produce guaranteed pussy upon mention. Only they never hear them; they usually have to translate dysfunctional behavior into straightforward lingo. In other words, they'll realize that sitting around for eight hours waiting for someone who has mysteriously disappeared from the studio means that particular someone fell into some pussy.

Then there were my absolute favorites - artists who've yet to release any music and still have managers. In English, that means they smoke too much weed to answer a phone or use a computer, don't possess an iota of social skill, and think they're more relevant than they really are. However, in all of my years playing bumper cars in the rap game theme park, unnecessary networking was the by far most prevalent and cumbersome idiosyncrasy.

Yo Zone man, I'mma holla at you son, we definitely gonna get up! Yo gimme your math, I'mma get at you, we gotta connect, we gotta build, we gotta politic for real.

My experiences at Vee-Dubbs with characters like the YGz and Midnight and my days running with Davian trained me to be a man of my word and cut to the chase. After all, time is irreplaceable; nothing you can tell someone is worse than wasting their time. Every minute wasted is a dollar lost, so he who wastes your time or he whose word no longer carries any weight should be treated the same as someone who stole every solitary dime you had in a Ponzi scheme.

It was good speaking with you Zone, I'll see you when I see you, good luck.

I think if I heard someone say that, I'd shoot a celebratory load in my pants. Why people feel the need to go beyond "hi" and "bye" in this business has always befuddled me. A good number of people working in fields of entertainment are there simply because they can't survive in any other walk of life. More often than not, they're too irresponsible to start a business, too aloof to hold a nine-to-five, and too lazy to pursue a career with skill training requirements. Therefore, expecting your time to be respected is like expecting no lines and multiple open tellers at a post office in a black neighborhood.

BLOWIN' SMOKE

"ZONE, can you do the November edition of Beat Society at the Knitting Factory?"

It was Stef Tataz, the event organizer for Beat Society. Stef and I go back to the late '90s; Beat Society is a producer showcase. I never was one for showcases, but sometimes you just want to gauge your latest material over a loud system in a room full of people. My career was in a slump in late 2004 and I needed all the feedback I could get. Every time I play beats for a room full of average hip-hop fans, they just stand there perplexed, not knowing if its utterly amazing, absolute garbage, or just…strange. Nonetheless, it was always funny to see folks' reactions.

"You have a different sound," Stef went on in a continued effort to persuade me. "I think it'll give the event some diversity."

Fuck it. Two other producers (my boys Slopfunkdust and Marco Polo) took the stage with me at the Knitting Factory NYC on Saturday, November 13th, 2004. The crowd didn't know how to swallow me on stage in a full-length fur coat and playing the most bizarre shit I had, but every now and then I struck a nerve and got a head nod wave. A nod from Just Blaze (who was the producer of all producers at the moment) gave my confidence a caffeine shot and I began to roll. That is, until the rapper-performs-live-over-the-producers'-beats portion of the event.

Sean Price is a veteran MC from NYC's Boot Camp Clik; he was one of the MCs chosen for the event. His label A&R, Dru-Ha, joined him onstage. The BCC were responsible for a good chunk of what I was listening to in the mid-'90s. Sean was also being managed by my cousin, Cynical, and had a raw sense of humor like I did. Cynical would often mention us working on a joint effort.

"You two crazy, funny-ass niggas would be a perfect fit," she told me one afternoon at her Brooklyn apartment. "People would eat that shit up." I never got the chance to hear Sean over my music until that night. It sounded dope, but it didn't last long.

"Yo, turn that beat off."

It was Dru-Ha. For whatever reason, he felt the need to chime in with an opinion. Marco played a beat. Slop played a beat. On my next go round, Sean rapped all of 15 seconds before I heard a repeat request from Dru-Ha.

Oh well. J-Zone is an acquired taste. I came up in the '80s and early '90s, when "haters" didn't exist, just opinions. If someone thought you sucked, they said it; you had a right to disagree and you kept it moving. Dru was entitled to his opinion and I respected his opinion fully. Shit, his honesty was refreshing to me. However, something bizarre happened 30 minutes later. I heard someone calling my name after the event was over, as I was stuffing my MPC-2000 drum machine into my duffel bag.

"You J-Zone? What's up man I'm Dru-Ha, I'm the A&R at Duck Down Records."

Huh?

"Take my business card; I keep hearing you and Sean have a lot in common. I never heard your shit, but people keep telling me you're dope. You and Sean should do an album together. Holla at me, we should build."

Let me reach for the pause button so I can reanalyze this. My music is apparently so ill-fitting that you tell me to refrain from playing beats while your artist is on stage. Thirty minutes later, you're here schlepping business cards and attempting to discuss me and the said artist engaging in a full-length collaborative effort? Gotcha Mr. Ha, I just wanted to clarify that.

I don't have a follicle of shame admitting that my music wasn't flying off shelves at the time. To be honest, I was on my way down. All attempts to revive a bedridden career aside, Sean Price was super dope and whoever told Dru that we'd be a good fit was probably onto something. I swallowed the Beat Society snub and looked at it as an opportunity. If you're running out of fuel on the Loop Parkway in Long Island (the epitome of a helpless feeling), you're not going to refuse a gas can from a person who doesn't like the type of car you're driving.

The phone number on Dru's business card didn't work, but somehow I got in touch with him. After a phone conversation, we agreed to meet. Frankly, I was curious about how he would react to my music in a private meeting as opposed to in a crowded club. Constructive criticism in the music business is like money your ex owes you - you never see it.

Unfortunately, my moment of truth never came. After confirming our 3:30 meeting in Manhattan via phone at noon, I took the 75 minute one-way commute to 23rd Street that all Southeast Queens residents dread - in the pouring rain.

"Dru isn't here and won't be back for the rest of the day," someone in his office told me as I stood there looking utterly stupid and feet-soaked through a flimsy pair of Asics. "He went to give a lecture at White Plains High School."

Superb. A phone call from Mr. Ha to cancel our meeting would've saved me time (and money), but how could I be so loony as to expect someone in the music business to actually respect my fuckin' time? As I prepared for my return commute home, I had an epiphany - I'd rather fail on my own than "holla" at half-steppers to collaborate, build, and connect so we can fail in unison and frolic in a steaming pile of dung.

NOW What?

It's now summer 2010. The music business as we know it (particularly from a hip-hop standpoint) is squirming on the floor, writhing in pain. A new day is coming. Only a handful will be able to adapt to life on land after living underwater for eons. Standing in a Baptist church-hot Fat Beats Record store in the West Village as they prepare to close their doors and end an era creates an aura of ambivalence for me. The end of the music biz as I know it obviously invokes some nostalgia, but the ghost of grandpa Herbie causes the moment-of-truth-seeker in me to start grinning from ear to ear.

"So where do we go from here?" asked a thirty-something hip-hop fan to nobody in particular. To my chagrin, the genuine and hard-working artists will struggle financially and have to find new ways adapt and retool. But when I thought of everyone that tried to surface level "holla", "build", and "politic" with me over the years, I couldn't help it - I had to laugh.

"To the employment agencies or back to the drawing board," I responded, partly in sarcasm and partly in seriousness. I recalled all of the phony, sweaty, and thoroughly sloppy people I met over the years who wasted my fuckin' time and tried to sell me previously blown grenades in this business. Entertainment gave them purpose, because entertainment promotes dysfunctional behavior. It's exciting. People love to see Kanye have an ego-maniacal meltdown, T.I. blooper his way back to jail, or Rapper X arrive onstage two hours late, stumbling over his own feet, and as high as a cross-continental 767. An irresponsible code of conduct is hilarious until your records aren't selling, you can't get booked, and a whole generation of young kids no longer gives a fuck who you are. Deep down, a twisted part of me loves, loves, loves the fact that the business side of the rap game is dying. Envisioning these overgrown little kids I've encountered actually dealing with the real world gets me excited. The thought of these disingenuous, head-in-the-clouds-ass rappers and dollar store moguls applying for crappy nine-to-fives is so God damn pleasant that it damn near makes me come. I remember hearing this Rapanese phrase pretty often:

Yo Zone, I'll definitely pay you the rest of the money for those beats, I'mma holla at you this week son.

There's no 365-day invoice period when you owe someone money in a life of crime. You or a loved one will just get murdered, that's it. The entertainment world is the only one I'm aware of where you're an asshole for expecting to be paid for your services or product. In the small pond of indie rap, the average artist will hear:

Yo man, give me a free beat or a free verse for the love of hip-hop.

Nigga please. Go into Wendy's and ask for a free Baconator "for the love of Trans fat" and see where it gets you. I'd like to think that the average musician makes music for the love. Passion is the motor that powers every good artist. But if you're aiming to get paid off work I did for "the love", you're smoking up your rent money.

Yo fam, meet me at 2PM at the studio.

A scheduled 2PM delivery for your job at Domino's Pizza cannot be delivered at 5:30 because you stopped to blaze some trees or go see your baby's mother. A 1PM arrival to 9AM meeting at your job is really a 3PM arrival at the unemployment office.

Yo my bad for not calling you back Zone, shit got mad hectic. I'mma holla at you soon though.

If you're absolutely positive that you can't work for "The Man" and you aspire to start your own business, I'd like to see you get "mad hectic" (read: high, drunk, or waist deep in some pussy) when you need to mail off your quarterly business taxes by a certain date. Look Einstein, it's not like when you forget to pay your T-Mobile bill and they shut down your cell phone. (Rappers and disconnected phones is a chapter in itself.) You're fucking with the IRS (also known as I Run Shit), so explain it to them when they bury your business. I can see some of the clowns I've encountered in this business trying to doggy paddle in the real world today:

What do you mean I can't pay my mortgage in $10 installments over 90 years? I paid for beats that way. Sorry Mr. Accountant, I can't find the FICA tax coupon that you sent me. Niggas came over for 40s and blunts and the shit just came up missing.

Hey dick, you're no longer the great shark you once were. Don't get it twisted, though. When you're forced to enter the real world and actually do what you say, say what you mean, arrive on time, and not waste people's time, you'll still be a shark. However, you'll be on land. Your business card is now only good for squashing a bug on the wall and not getting guts on your fingers. "Holla" at that piss test, potna.

12. FREQUENT FLYER MILES

It's one thing to perform for five people in a slop bucket in your hometown. It's a whole other ball of wax to get a taste of festivals, tours, and even five person crowds in slop buckets in places overseas. If it weren't for Europe, Japan, and Australia, both your favorite artist and I would've been in trouble eons ago.

In April of 2000, I lost my international travel cherry with a two week trip to Australia for a five date tour. Six months later, I went to Europe for the first time and stayed out there for three weeks. The moment my return flight home taxied down the runway at JFK Airport after that first European tour, I realized how much of a shit pit America is.

U.S. Customs agents loved to piss hot lemonade on my parade, most likely because I had every page in my passport filled with stamps from places they'd never see. If a young black man sporting cornrows and a football jersey is returning from Iceland, something strange is going on.

The agents used to take blades and cut up the fur coat I wore as a stage costume, looking for dope (or so they once said). Conversely, the customs agents in Europe would be almost too pleasant, merely asking me why I was in their country and telling me to enjoy my stay. That generally unwelcoming atmosphere at home and generally pleasant one abroad didn't only apply to airports. The very same theory transferred over to my actual shows.

I would typically exit stages from shows in my hometown to crowds full of aspiring artists with moderate to extreme halitosis handing me CD-R demos. My 'U.S. fan base' gradually became fellow artists looking to collaborate. Meanwhile, I would exit stages overseas to fans who had spent import prices to acquire my elusive and scarcely distributed albums. I guess the fact that fans were actually still fans overseas blew me away. It was enough to boost my morale when nobody in my neighborhood was listening to me because I hadn't done a song with Bang 'Em Smurf yet. Nonetheless, people in Copenhagen, Denmark were listening. Although I couldn't brag about that in the typical black barber shop, it gave me a private sense of hope. My constant compare and contrast of the American artist's experiences abroad and at home became known as what I call "The Jackson Theory." Overseas, people made you feel like Michael Jackson; at home, people made you feel like Tito Jackson.

Sleazy Listening

The pinnacle of my international travel experience was undoubtedly the Sleazy Listening European tour of October 2004, for two reasons. First and foremost, the line-up was somewhat anathema of what promoters and fans go for in America. J-Zone, Vakill, Louis Logic, and DJ Equal sharing the bill for 20 shows wouldn't ride here; none of us were famous enough to entice promoters outside of the major cities to shell out decent loot. Another reason the tour stood out was because it dispelled the perplexing segregation of rap that fell into place sometime in the '90s.

I recall reading *Word Up!* Magazine circa 1990 and noticing that a wild mixture of artists had just toured together: Freshco & Miz, Ice Cube, Too $hort, D-Nice, and Intelligent Hoodlum. Stylistically, the aforementioned artists represent apples, grapes, bananas, tomatoes, and kumquats. It was 100 percent feasible for a goofy and somewhat gimmicky group like The Afros to be on the same bill with a serious black radical artist like Paris, because there are only two types of rap - dope and wack. Somewhere along the line, the landscape of rap became subdivided by style ("thug rap," "nerd rap," "jiggy rap," "backpacker rap," etc.). Once that happened, the thought of me sharing a bill with a more street and commercially viable artist like N.O.R.E. seemed far-fetched. N.O.R.E. and I are two funny and politically incorrect artists who talk a lot of shit. Why wouldn't it work? Because in the early 2000s, many listeners felt most comfortable when they were able to place a sub-genre-labelled post-it note on your head. Backpacker. Take it and go. When I used to publicly express my desire to produce a song for a west coast-based and commercially viable artist like E-40 (which I eventually did), fans and critics said I was out of my skull because I make "backpacker rap." I was told that "backpacker rap" is any sample-based rap music that doesn't sell and nobody gets shot in the song lyrics.

Most fans of "thug rap" in 2004 weren't trying to hear my quirky beats or me rapping about something as soft as masturbating. Thus, I never got love on the streets. Conversely, most of my supposed "backpacker rap" demographic liked my production and my self-effacing approach, but they couldn't deal with me handling my relationship woes via my music, which came out as a constant feed of profanity-laced bitch-baiting and lambasting of the opposite sex. Why the fuck couldn't I talk shit about broads and do it over some artsy-fartsy funk beats? My grandfathers showed me how being dual-natured and misunderstood creates a mystique, but in the case of my career, that approach made shit that much more difficult for me.

As a result of these emerging rap rules and regulations, I fell into an unidentifiable sub-niche and I was nearly impossible to market for American tours. No matter who I was on the bill with, I was told by booking agents, "Their fans won't like you and your fans won't like them." I laughed at that statement, until I found that the only successful J-Zone shows in America were the ones where I performed alone. I didn't have a big enough crowd draw to continually do that.

So here we had four stooges that couldn't be any more different and we were getting ready to share a tour bill for an entire month. Louis was a conceptually ambitious and extremely eclectic artist, who little kids often mistook for Lenny Kravitz in airports. Both Lou and I would make songs about broads, but he would pen a heartfelt tune about a relationship. My girl song would be about how this bitch I knew was way too big to be wearing a God damn halter top. Lou had a romantic side, so he also had a female audience. I didn't have an iota of romance in my game, thus I was appealing solely to female inhabitants of Jupiter.

Vakill was from the South Side of Chicago and could probably bench press a Jeep Wrangler. He rapped one way - hard. However, like my rap partner Al-Shid, Va was extremely intelligent and witty and it put him far over the heads of the average hoodlums who listened to street rap in our era of "coloring inside the lines".

DJ Equal (a young turntable wizard from North Carolina) was still in his teens, a strict vegetarian, and the consummate hippie. Vakill needed a T-bone steak with a bowl of oatmeal.

"This should be fun," I said to myself on the flight to London to start the tour. "We're too different, somebody's gonna get their ass booed each night." How the fuck would this work for almost an entire month? I flashed back to two months prior, when I shared the bill with Immortal Technique for the ten-year-anniversary show for Fat Beats in Amsterdam. Could indie rap's self-made revolutionary and indie rap's self-made court jester headline a show together? Not in New York. Nonetheless, the show was an all out smash. The fact that we were in Europe probably had something to do with that two-sided appreciation coin.

As for Sleazy Listening, the 25 days and 20 shows that followed my moment of doubt on the plane went over without one single hitch. Four impossible to categorize and relatively obscure misfits at home went abroad and felt like mega-stars on a nightly basis. Roughly three percent of the packed to capacity crowd at the sizable venue in Seville, Spain knew who any of us were, but four Americans came to their town and left it all on stage; that equaled an

european tour flyers

animated show of crowd appreciation. I never saw a response of that magnitude anywhere elsewhere in my 12 years of performing as an artist and DJ. It was then we all realized that we weren't as different from each other as fans, promoters, and journalists back home had made us feel. We also gained a new appreciation for each others' music in very comedic fashion.

After the first two or three shows of the tour, Lou and I suggested to Vakill that he do a catchy tag line to get the crowd going. He needed a trademark.

All my ladies in the house! If your pussy is clean, let me hear you scream!

Lou and I were backstage listening to Va be unintentionally hilarious by greeting crowds rife with innocent-looking and thoroughly scared white girls with that line every show for the rest of the tour. When we got to Larvik, Norway and saw the crowd from behind the dressing room curtain, Lou pulled me aside.

"Jay, you think Va is gonna say that shit tonight?" Lou asked, almost sarcastically.

"Hell yeah that crazy nigga is gonna say that shit," I responded, my voice bloated with anticipation. "And when he does, I'm gonna be rollin'!"

"But look at the crowd!" Lou responded, like I should intervene and tell Va not to say his new catchphrase.

"That's even better!" I said. "Fuck it!"

You could hear dust hit the floor when Va dropped his call and response on a crowd of the youngest, skinniest, blondest, most blue-eyed European girls I've ever seen. Sleazy Listening was somehow booked for a Norwegian all-ages event, and a room full of teenage Barbie dolls just got a call for clean pussy pride from a brother who was built like he was hanging with D-Bo and muscling bikes in the hood. Va was also wearing a hoodie with a silk screen of warrior head dripping blood on it. The whole exchange was comparable to Mr. T telling one of the daughters from *Full House*, "If you douche and you know it, clap your hands... fool!"

The Sleazy Listening experience brought us from London, to Austria, to Germany, and parts in between. It made me flashback to 1999, when I had to be forced into becoming a live performer. If I hadn't taken the plunge, I would've missed out on the greatest 25 consecutive days of my entire life. At the end of it all, I was flying home with a wallet full of cash that I couldn't fold, a lifetime of memories, and a dramatic boost in confidence. The money went into the bank and the memories are spilling into this book, but the confidence died after about a week. My return to the states meant that I was back to being Tito Jackson again. Thank you, Europe.

dour festival, belgium (2006)

13. THE CHITLIN' CIRCUIT

My international travel itinerary didn't always include extremely fuckable women, a booming merchandise table, a decent show fee, and hilariously awkward public ploys for clean pussy. Things across seas got downright Snooki (ugly) at times. In the world of indie rap, a number of artists do shows on good faith, often bypassing the paperwork and waiting until the night of performance to get paid. Sometimes you got your money and sometimes this lax business practice bit you square in the ass, but the one no-no was agreeing to shows overseas without paperwork and flights purchased in advance. Ensuring that the promoters weren't fans who didn't understand that our livelihoods were at stake was essential. Al-Shid, my European Tour DJ Jazz T, and I had to learn the hard way that even this protocol wasn't fool proof. The French promoter who left us stranded in Nantes, France had to learn the hard way what a fear-fueled foreign luxury tax extorting felt like. Go ahead and say that we didn't spend the last few euros we each had to our names to buy train tickets to hunt his ass down instead of going back to Charles De Gaulle Airport and waiting 24 hours for our trip home. Go ahead and deny that the sound of Shid tossing him down a flight of stairs sounded like a Buddy Rich drum solo. But Milli Vanilli can tell you how true it was that we got our money and learned that promoters overseas can and will use the language barrier to short you out of your earnings. They'll also tell you how taxing it is to have been jerked, have no money, and be assed-out in the countryside of a land where you don't speak the language.

Still, more often than not, shows overseas made shows at home feel like jury duty. There was one particular stretch of shows that I did throughout the South-Atlantic region of the U.S. that I always refer to as the Chitlin' Circuit Tour, Summer 2005.

"ZONE, your record isn't doing well at all; you'd better hit the road."

A sales rep from Fat Beats (my primary music distributor) was on my ass again.

"You have to get a presence in U.S. markets outside of California and

New York, your SoundScan numbers are pretty brutal."

My latest effort, *A Job Ain't Nuthin' but Work*, was an abysmal failure in the sales department. My popularity had been on a steady decline over the years and I hadn't established much of a U.S. fan base outside of the major markets. I needed to shake the post-European tour depression I was enduring, and a run of shows might do me some good. I agreed to seven gigs and hit the road. Before I could leave though, my car decided to menstruate. There was no way I was about to floor the hooptie through cross-burning land, so my pops drove me to Port Authority to take a Greyhound Bus to and through the south to rock the few venues that would put me on the bill.

When the bus pulled in to the station at Fredericksburg, Virginia, I had to drain the boa constrictor. The toilets on the bus didn't work and the driver had consequently taped the bathroom door shut.

"We'll be taking a 10 minute break," the driver lied through the bus intercom. "The bus will be pulling out of the station at 4:05."

I hopped off the bus at 3:55 and ran to the bathroom in the rest stop, which was about 45 feet from where the bus was parked. I was the only person to go into the building, so what does our slow, country bumpkin bus driver say to himself?

Fuck it, one high-yellow monkey don't stop no show.

I was in the midst of a Colt 45 40 ounce piss when I glanced through the bathroom window and saw the bus pull out of the station - at 3:58. I was still leaking all over my cargo shorts and down my leg when I attempted to flag the fleeing, rapper-less bus down, but as it turned onto Route 1 and cruised southbound into the distance, my high school sprinter speed failed me. My knee suddenly told me to fuck off and I collapsed into a motionless human mass on a hot Virginia sidewalk, still peeing on myself. My merchandise, my clothes, my trademark fur coat, and my cassette copies of Tweedy Bird Loc's *187 Ride By* and No Face's *Wake Your Daughter Up* were all en route to Richmond on that bus. I lay there face down for about three minutes in disbelief, creating a perfect photo op for a greeting card for failure.

I wanted to cry like a teenage valley girl with a zit and fall into a slumber on the asphalt, but I was startled by the sound of a Mack truck rolling by and the stench of it spewing an exhaust cloud over me. I lay there another three minutes feeling half dead, before I gathered myself, hopped to my feet, and wiped the granules of concrete off my face. My habit of always keeping my keys, wallet, and cell phone on me saved my ass; within 30 minutes, I was bumming a ride to Richmond with the opening act for that night's show. Pentagon-level security from Greyhound saved also my ass; the promoter was able to just walk onto the bus and grab all of my shit off the racks when it pulled into the Richmond station. After that quagmire, I was ready to give the performance of a lifetime.

Giving the performance of a lifetime is a bit difficult with four spectators in a venue that holds 400 people. I tried like hell, though. The four Richmond patrons weren't paying me any mind, so I decided to leave the stage and perform my whole show in the middle of the floor space. They still ignored me, but when the microphone began to feedback due to me being in front of the speakers with it, they finally showed some sense of giving a fuck and the otherwise disinterested quartet yelled for me to "go the fuck back onto the stage." The whole time I was praying they'd boo me, but unfortunately they didn't give enough of a fuck to.

The college towns would've been much better turnouts for me, but there was one small problem - it was the beginning of July, nobody was in school. Oops. Chapel Hill, North Carolina had about eight spectators, but at least they were live. Five lucky people got to see me in Wilmington, North Carolina, but one of them was a diehard fan. About 30 people stayed for my set in Springfield, Virginia (where the venue's capacity was 500) but at least my cousin Tony showed up. The venue in Johnson City, Tennessee was reminiscent of someone's living room, a bar that kept the houselights on for the entire night. However, five of the nine people at that show had driven in from Nashville (which is on the other side of the state) to see me. In Asheville, North Carolina, there was an issue with my hotel and I was forced to stay in the guest bedroom at the promoter's house. As I lay on a linen-less mattress with an icepack on my jammed up knee and watched the house cat rummage through my duffel bag, I called up a friend to see if my slowly-emerging thoughts that it might be time to inch in a new musical direction were warranted.

"You're getting guarantees though, aren't you?" he asked me. A lot of artists have the whole guaranteed show money thing fucked up. Yes, guarantees are the only way to go, but the value of a show is beyond cash. The most important aspect of touring is acquiring new fans, period. When the house is packed, the perception of you is greater, there's more room to convert new fans, promoters want you back, and your merchandise sales increase. The whole purpose is to set things up in Bumblefuck City so you can come back next year and demand more money, get a better hotel, and perform to a sea of new faces who got wind of you wrecking shop the last time you were there. It's all about growth; I was chasing buses, sleeping on bare mattresses, and getting a reputation for shirt-eating (albeit entertaining) shows in the world of promoters. My name was bird shit when it came to turnouts. My guarantees didn't pay much, but I much rather would have performed for packed houses for even less. Whether it was the fault of my decline in popularity, shoddy promotion, or just bad timing, I don't know. Nonetheless, I was never invited back to that region.

On the 21-hour bus ride home from Johnson City, I had a lot of time to think. Thinking kept my mind off that living room couch of a broad sitting next to me with the Jheri curl eating a mayonnaise sandwich in the summer heat. It was during that never-ending ride that I entertained the idea of life after the music business for the very first time. I took a look around at my fellow 28-year-olds from college; I saw stability, which I didn't have. Of course I could sleep 'til noon and got to travel to Denmark for work, so there was a definite trade off in the level of excitement that I was experiencing. However, I was also paying for my own health insurance, unsure of where from and when my next check was coming, and after bills, there wasn't much left. The money I made over the course of those seven shows got me through a few bills, but if I hadn't gained any new fans, sold any CDs, or been invited back to do more shows, the entire experience was moot. My grievous pondering was interrupted by some new bus passengers.

That's what I'm talkin' bout, my nigga. Blood up!

Greyhound's Pentagon level of security was back at it again. The bus stopped in Baltimore, Maryland and picked up five dressed-to-the-tee members of the Bloods gang. They let the whole bus know that the Crips were about to have problems when they touched down in the Rotten Apple. One of them began to toy with his switchblade as he sat down next to a woman and her infant son. It was time to get a new car too; the bus was a dangerous place. One of the other Bloods sat next to me.

"Far Rock, that's what's up my nigga, I heard they got Bloods out that muthafucka," he said with a pre-pussy gettin' excitement. My burgeoning hobby as a high school basketball reporter had gotten me some perks, like free t-shirts from the schools I went to for games. Big Boss Blood had no idea that the shirt I was wearing was merely a Far Rockaway High School gym shirt that the school's athletic director had given me at a game. I had no affiliation with the Bloods in one of Queens' roughest neighborhoods. I wasn't inclined to tell him that though, so he waxed poetic for 15 minutes about the importance of Crab (Crip) killing. And they say backpacker rap artists don't come near the streets.

I never thought I'd make it home from the Chitlin' Circuit tour, but I finally limped through the door at 5AM on a Tuesday. The rest of the world was preparing to board the iron horse and trudge to their square jobs, but not this low-level rapper. I plopped down on the bed feeling more physically and mentally drained than I had ever felt in my entire life. My brain went back to pondering if this was something to continue doing into my 30s; my heart said to keep plugging. I had worked too hard and sacrificed too much to quit like a chump because of a slump. The handful of people that showed appreciation during the Chitlin' Circuit tour symbolized hope. Then again, my next show in NYC literally had a whopping two spectators on hand, one of whom was a childhood friend. He wanted to see what this illustrious J-Zone thing I continually spoke of was all about.

A phone call from Fat Beats interrupted my deep slumber at 11AM, with the voice on the other end informing me that my recent remix album (*Gimme Dat Beat Fool*) had failed and neither the stores nor the fans seemed to give a shit.

"Fuck it, who cares?" I dribbled into the phone, before hanging up mid-argument and going back to sleep. The next day I'd keep plugging though, because real artists never quit. Or do they?

14. RISE & SLIP

My romp through the music biz took me from the land of promising up-and-coming hip-hop multi-talents to a dairy fridge at Wal-Mart - where a special edition carton of Lactaid serves as my latest billboard. The in-between phase of "blowing up" never came, but that missing piece doesn't bother me these days. It was a fun ride, though at times I'm bewildered by my complete loss of interest in something that engulfed my life for 25 years over the course of two. In 2001 though, I was on my way.

Creepin' On Ah Come-up

I trumped *Music for Tu Madre* and my second album (2000's *A Bottle of Whup Ass*) with the release of *Pimps Don't Pay Taxes*, an album that's regarded by all 17 people familiar with my catalog as my magnum opus. Rummaging through old family photo albums had paid off; I unearthed the picture of my great uncles that graced the album cover and inspired the title. As a producer, I had come a long way from my 1995 Pete Rock knockoffs. My archive of VHS tapes crammed with old TV shows and B movies coupled with my penchant for making something funky out of the un-funkiest records in the galaxy - like Hawaiian LPs that other producers wouldn't use for a game of Frisbee - gave me a strong underground following and my own sound. Freelance production work was trickling in and I began seeing my beats on other people's albums. When Biz Markie bought a beat from me for his *Weekend Warrior* album, I knew I had some shit.

As an artist, I wasn't far off from my rapping idols Too $hort, Eazy-E, Tim Dog, and The Afros; I went for entertainment value over precision. My cohorts, Huggy and Al-Shid, were building fan bases that rivaled mine. The former was an extremely gifted writer with a unique off the wall stream of consciousness style and the latter penned a caliber of multi-layered punch lines that I hadn't heard since Common's *Resurrection* album. More importantly, Huggy and Shid were as hard to pigeonhole in 2001 as I was.

A large percentage of Huggy's fans just happened to be nutzoid conspiracy theorists, who chewed my ear off about the book *Behold A Pale Horse*

at shows when he wasn't around. What his fans failed to realize was that Hug was probably the most thorough and versatile artist out of all of us.

Shid was another intriguing cat. He had a rep for brazenly rushing rappers on stage fully intoxicated with a King Kong-sized chip on his shoulder, looking to battle. He'd also knuckled down a turkey or two for rubbing him the wrong way at shows. With all Shid lacked in the decorum department though, he was so clever as an MC that you couldn't merely write him off as a goon. I still say that he was the most naturally gifted MC I've ever worked with, but his penchant for confrontation sometimes formed a lunar eclipse over his wit and skill.

We were all stylistically different from each other, so nothing that we did collectively (as the Old Maid Billionaires) was supposed to work. The slap-dash and promotionally-challenged release methods of my first three albums were sure ways to fail in the music business at the time. My self-deprecating tales of jerking off to Lucy Liu pictures after a fruitless night of trying to get some pussy were frivolous compared to the battle rap and thug-isms that most of my peers were into. Furthermore, that goofiness wasn't supposed to work on an album where the next song was a Shid solo ditty about him slapping the shit out of a bitch-ass nigga and burying him 30 feet in the ground. After Shid's soliloquy of doom, Hug would chime in with a song about the fraudulence of organized religion. Miraculously, it all sounded cohesive.

Musically, my choice of samples wasn't supposed to work either. I recall going record shopping with Pete Rock once. He shook his head when I grabbed a Korean record with some sailboats on the album cover.

"Zone, you on that other shit, I can't fuck with that," was what arguably the greatest hip-hop producer of all time told me. I took the record home and made a beat that became the backdrop for one of my most popular songs. I recalled being hinged to cables and harnesses in New Rochelle hospital and marveling at how the Threat album excelled on heavy helpings of tired P-Funk samples; I took the same theory and reversed the resources.

The Old Maid slogan became *Fuckin' up Hip-Hop since 1998*, and it lived via silk-screen on the back of our first run of t-shirts. We were still courting a niche audience, but people with major clout began to take notice. In 2002, Atlantic Records placed a multi-album deal on the table. The label A&R suggested that I "make a few songs for the club, get a few beats from other producers, and focus on being a rapper," more so due to my personality than my rapping skill. He wasn't sold on the OMB thing, but I was making good enough money independently to survive without a day job and turned down the deal. We created enough of a stir to obtain CD distribution through BMG, a major player in getting independent music placed in Tower Records, Virgin Megastore, and Best Buy. A presence in the major chains was the difference between U.S. Polo Association and Polo when it came to legitimizing artists.

The OMBs now had a viable chance of breaking into the "middle ground" music scene. That was a place where you could take a rogue approach to music, but finally tell your relatives in Barnyard, Oklahoma that they can find your CD at the local mall instead of you e-mailing them links to specialty websites. With all the shake-ups the OMBs were creating though, I peeled open the can in late 2001 and the whole operation blew up in my face.

Tension had been bubbling in the crew like a Miami Bass 808 for about a year. Trouble in Old Maid land shouldn't have been a surprise. Problems will inevitably be waiting like debt collectors on a land line answering machine when you're young, green to the business, and overlooking the importance of communication.

I recalled watching Leaders of the New School (one of my favorite childhood rap groups) break up live on *Yo! MTV Raps* in 1993. I wondered why they couldn't just keep it together for the sake of the music. As fans, we don't see the friction that ignites when multiple chefs stir a pot. The gumbo is good, the restaurant patrons love it, but one muthafucka would've replaced paprika with turmeric and now there's drama in the kitchen. Sam and Dave purportedly loathed each other, but they got on stage every night to croon the hits. EPMD's break-up was one of the most tumultuous in music history, but they eventually got back together.

That future olive branch for the sake of music never came for the OMBs. In early 2002, we split due to irreparable and constant creative friction, but maintained the mutual respect we had for each other. I continued to work with Shid sporadically until the day I retired, but the makeshift trio of rule-breakers was no more. The majority of my time in the business that followed our split was spent trying to win dunk contests with good ideas and a torn meniscus.

J-ZONE'S FIRST AND ONLY TOP 50 BILLBOARD CHART APPEARANCE (#39, 2001) AND MAGAZINE COVER (VAPORS, 2003)

SLiPPiN' SOLO

Surviving in the rap world as a solo artist with no affiliations and a "no rules" mentality was equivalent to growing up in the hood with no knuckle game. The crew approach gave three individually hard-to-market artists a vehicle to make everything work. There's been a safety in numbers policy in place in hip-hop since the '90s' inception of major crews (i.e. Wu-Tang, Death Row, Cash Money, Boot Camp, Def Jux, Native Tongues, Hieroglyphics, Stonesthrow, Dipset, etc.) But when you're forced to embark on a solo career without branding and affiliation, your chances of making an impact drop like Barack Obama's midterm stock. Hug's depth and political conscience and Shid's confrontational edge balanced out my class clown act, as many stratospheres apart as they were.

Dick $tallion and Contakt stayed on board to help me revamp the live show and the approach, but by 2003 I was making comedy rap with very little thuggish confrontation and negligible amounts of seriousness. The albums that followed *Pimps Don't Pay Taxes* (2003's *$ick Of Bein' Rich* and 2004's *A Job Ain't Nuthin' but Work*) were more like Skillet & Leroy records than indie rap records. The production morphed into a new variation on my original sound, I returned to rapping and learned to love it (I had no choice), I began to acquire the guest services of artists I had grown up admiring (King Tee, Masta Ace, Devin The Dude, and J-Ro from Tha Alkaholiks), I finally had major distribution, and I even hired publicists to help establish the new me. The adjustments were equivalent to The Gap's change of logo in 2010. When something is technically better, it doesn't necessarily mean it's aesthetically better. More than half of my fans were disappointed in my post-*Pimps* work, and I began to jog in quicksand with a rep as a burgeoning novelty act.

I had an opportunity to interview Too $hort for London's *Hip-Hop Connection* magazine in 2003; he gave me a side piece of artist advice.

"I made albums that sounded good after *Life Is...Too Short*," he said in his trademark drawl over the phone. "But it was all about getting popular on a national scale for the first time. You were that hungry new artist who was still getting a ride to the studio."

$hort had millions of fans. I, on the other hand, had a fraction of that. Losing as few as 100 fans could do some damage. By 2004, the damage was irreversible.

"Nobody gives a shit about J-Zone anymore, your fans grew up," a sales rep from Fat Beats once told me. "You're basically irrelevant as an artist."

I began to see first-hand why my childhood heroes No Face, Son of

97

Bazerk, and The Afros only made one album each. There was nowhere for them to go in a business built on labeling and closest common denominator categorizing. By 2004, rap segregation had become ten times more rigid than it was in 1990.

I was constantly being told by the sales reps that I needed to back door my way into other artist's fan bases via collaboration. Additionally, they had to be artists who were making major noise in the indie rap scene. According to them, there was no way to market a class clown rapper with odd-sounding beats who was too misogynistic for Atmosphere fans, too goofy for Saigon fans, and made seven different remixes of Project Pat's "Gel & Weave" in his spare time. People tend to ignore something that they can't categorize.

When *A Job Ain't Nuthin but Work* flopped, I lost my major distribution deal and went back to manufacturing my own shit. Having my CDs in major chain stores was great for legitimacy reasons, but a placebo as far as all else was concerned. With no real money to shoot a quality video and no place to get it seen by the general public (YouTube was still a year away), there was no vehicle to support true indie records that were shelved next to major ones. Especially when they were $18.99 a pop and competing with CDs from more popular artists that were on sale for $11.99. (I begged my distributor to drop the prices on my albums with no luck.) With illegal downloading on the rise, the record business shot itself in the kneecaps by raising CD prices and indie artists with major distribution took it in the shitter. The J-Zone section in the major music chains was comparable to Barney Fife sharing a prison lunch table with Mr. T and Stanley "Tookie" Williams, as Juvenile and Kanye West were my alphabetical neighbors on either side. I should have called one of my albums *Please Kanye, Don't Hurt 'Em*. Obviously, when the main chain stores folded (between 2006 and 2008), pallets of unsold J-Zone product flew back in droves.

Instrumental projects were all the hip-hop rage in 2006. I just knew that mine - *Experienced!* and *To Love a Hooker*, a limited-edition nod to Hendrix and a soundtrack to a non-existent film, respectively - would give me a second wind as a producer and airlift me out of the novelty bin. Both albums had the impact of a *Ron Artest's Greatest Rap Hits* compilation. To this day, CDs of the latter pop up in my medicine cabinet, my car's glove compartment, and even behind my refrigerator. If I had as many hookers as I have unsold *To Love a Hooker* CDs , I'd make Fillmore Slim look like Lamar Latrell.

I hung up my artist hat in late 2006 and focused solely on DJing and producing. A record label summoned me to make an entire album with one of my favorite artists, but after driving 30 miles to the studio for scheduled sessions and being stood up for the fifth consecutive time, I got frustrated and left the ball in their court. I'm still waiting for a phone call about our next session or the reimbursement of my gas money.

Album sales in 2007 were strapped to the electric chair and artists could no longer afford to pay for beats. Additionally, chasing people down for a remaining $50 owed to me for old invoices was like trying to capture a nimble roach in a box of Raisin Bran. I was also being told regularly that my beats were hard to rap to because they sounded like porno music. Life imitated pigeonhole; I went on to score the music for a skin flick called *Asian Bang*. Believe me, it was better to set the soundtrack to a ho tramping out than it was to do it for someone rapping about rapping, but the pause for porn didn't help my full-blown reputation as some type of featherweight novelty act. DJing parties and gigs with my Australian DJ partner, DJ Sheep, afforded me the chance to continue traveling, having fun, and reinventing myself, but all of my new endeavors were either short-lived or not lucrative enough to pay bills.

I didn't see myself transforming into a curmudgeon, but those close to me had a front row seat. Irony reared its head in early 2007; the person to set indie rap's loudest misogynist straight was a woman.

"You no seems happy," my ex-girlfriend told me one day as we walked through the Green Acres Mall on the Queens-Long Island border. Her Japanese accent was heavy and her knowledge of the music biz was on par with a wino's knowledge of Bertrand's postulate math theorem. Sometimes opinions from folks on the outside are less inhibited by ulterior motive, though.

"You love the rap, but you hate the business," she keenly observed while we stood in Modell's looking at running sneakers. "You cannot have one without the other. It no make sense if you're no happy and not making living."

15. THE QUITTER

"PEOPLE don't get it, but that doesn't mean you should quit." - Danger Mouse

With all of the success Brian Burton (aka Danger Mouse) has had, it would've made sense to take heed when he told me that. It was Brian who called me up about my second album when it came out in May of 2000. Working at a small record store in Georgia at the time, he contacted me to discuss ordering it directly and we became good friends. Two years later, he recorded his album (with Jemini, a New York MC), *Ghetto Pop Life*, in my basement studio. At that point, we became music peers. In 2004, he went to Washington DC and threw a grenade into the U.S. Copyright Offices by merging samples from the 'you rap clowns better stay the fuck away from our catalog' Beatles' *White Album* and vocals from Jay-Z's *The Black Album*. The result was *The Grey Album*, a concoction that forever marked his spot in music history. A year after that, we were no longer music peers. I was still grinding it out and losing steam each year in the quickly dissolving indie rap scene, while he conversely shot into the remote universe of pop super-stardom. Despite our polarizing success stories, Brian and I always remained friends. He was cool enough to invite my D-List ass to roll with him to A-List events. Brian found it funny when my old crush, Lucy Liu, walked right past me and I didn't even notice her. I realized at one of those parties that Brian had become a legitimate celebrity without ever forgetting who he was; to this day I respect the shit out of him for it. Advice from a friend in a place like that usually isn't something you turn a deaf ear to.

"I get it, Cee-Lo [who formed pop group Gnarls Barkley with Brian] gets it, the people I play your stuff for get it," Brian told me while I was doing push-ups in the living room of his Jetsons-style pad in L.A. "But the average person just doesn't get it. They don't know if you're a funny dude who's just venting or if you're misogynist and ignorant."

The only other black man in the music industry as light-skinned as me (Brian and I could pass for brothers) was spot on. For as long I as I could re-call, I was an artist's artist and a producer's producer, but the average listener couldn't really digest what I was doing. Respect from my peers was gratifying, but as of late it wasn't giving me the Pistol Pete-like assists I needed to survive and boost my sense of accomplishment as a struggling 30-year-old musician.

Over the course of 2006 and 2007, I began my gradual self-imposed exile from the music business. My semi-retirement clause still allowed me to do shows outside of New York, because I hate turning down a chance to travel and get paid for it. By the end of '07 though, show offers had dried up. A promoter with a solid reputation booked me for a show in L.A. out of nowhere, so I jumped on it.

Brian brought a friend from *Mad TV* to the gig, a childhood idol of mine in DJ Bilal Bashir (Ice-T's producer) was DJing for me, and my friend Josh came through. I was in a reputable club with a dope stage and a huge room. The opening act brought through a giant contingent to support them; the house was Department of Motor Vehicles packed.

When I went to the restroom to take my routine, nerve-induced, pre-show shit, someone must have grabbed the mic and made the crowd aware of the 300 winning Lotto tickets outside on the sidewalk of Hollywood Blvd., because I came back to a completely empty room. By the time I hit the stage at midnight as the headliner, I had five spectators, all of whom were probably there by chance. A quick glance at that crowd revealed that they were texting and holding conversations amongst themselves during my set.

I was used to this, no big deal. I recalled the shows on my Chitlin' Circuit tour two years prior and just about every show I had done in America over the previous four years. Single digit turnouts never ever stopped me from doing my job, because I was just doing what I loved to do anyway. But three songs into the set, something bizarre happened and it happened in less than five seconds. I no longer gave a fuck, but not in the typical I-don't-give-a-fuck-about-offending-the-bitch-in-the-front-row-when-I-call-her-a-bitch way that I was accustomed to. This was utter disinterest.

All I could think about six songs into my 14-song set was where the fuck I was going to get dinner from. Then I thought about how I was missing a weekend of good games at the Nike IS8 high school basketball tournament in my neighborhood. I had an $85 parking ticket on my dresser that still had to be paid. Everything crossed my mind except the fact that I was on stage performing in Los Angeles, CA. The disconnect I felt while on stage that night could be compared to a Kardashian giving an acceptance speech in a room full of nuclear physicists.

Between songs, I told Bilal to clip four songs from the set so I could truncate this live funeral. The remaining 22 minutes still felt like four score and seven years. That night could only be likened to playing the last game of your

NBA career and you're down 130 points at halftime. You play for pride, you give onlookers a reason to respect you, but you look at hitting the showers with the same anticipation as you would a night with Stacey Dash. I gave every iota of energy I had to get through that set and when it was finally all over, I felt like I had just busted the mother of all nuts. Leaving the stage that night and knowing I'd never perform again gave me relief on the level of getting an HIV negative test result after a weekend of frolicking raw dog at a swinger party.

Unbeknownst to me, the career downsizing would be a process that would continue over another year. It would culminate at a point where I had zero interest or involvement in music whatsoever.

The Last Lap

Financially, I barely scraped by post-2006. I was without question the most frugal musician who ever lived, and that was the lone reason I somehow survived living in NYC while pulling in peanuts and clipping out coupons.

I seriously contemplated finding a Plan B. That plan entailed experimenting with everything from writing to teaching. I filmed nationally televised videos for Foot Locker stores, but I quit after they didn't want to pitch in $5 from their billion dollar corporate budget to reimburse me for travel expenses. I asked Foot Locker for a free pack of socks for allowing them to film videos of me acting like I gave a fuck about LeBron James' $12 sneakers that sold for $165. In response, they offered me a 25 percent discount on the socks. I'll bop through the South Side of Chicago wearing a mini-skirt and open-toed sandals before I shop in a God damn Foot Locker again.

I also went back to Purchase and taught a music course for two years. My students reminded me of myself working on *Music for Tu Madre* in that same building ten years prior. Momentarily, being around young and hungry musicians inspired me to get my punk ass back into the studio. The results came in the form of an unexpected creative brain fart in mid-2008. It was my final hip-hop hurrah.

Live @ the Liqua Sto revolved around the same St. Ides Malt Liquor rap commercials from the early '90s that traumatized me to bad beer. I summoned all of my rap homies to make guest appearances: Prince Paul, Celph Titled, Al-Shid, Louis Logic, RA the Rugged Man, and others. I even tried video promotion for the first time (with a series of hilarious YouTube vignettes and music videos) and can't recall having that much fun with a record since the *Music for Tu Madre* days.

The survival side painted a different portrait. I was completely irrelevant to both the hip-hop world and the general public. *Pimps Don't Pay Taxes* sold about 5,000 physical copies in its first month for sale in 2001. *Live @ the Liqua Sto* sold 46 copies (physical and digital combined) in its first month for sale in 2008.

In December of that same year, I went into the basement, grabbed a stack of records, and went to turn on my sampler like I had done just about every day for the last 16 years. I didn't feel up to it though, so I took a few days off. The days turned into weeks, but I didn't miss making music. I literally forced myself to make some beats the following month, because at the end of the day, music was a job – stop bitchin' and get your ass in the studio. Forcing the issue didn't work.

I had recently landed my first beat on a major label release (The Lonely Island's "Santana DVX" featuring E-40) after a decade of grinding in relative obscurity. The fact that "J-Zone of all people" (as quoted from a review of the album) was chosen to be on such a commercially viable and high profile album was equally as shocking as it was cool. The Lonely Island score was a hell of a high note, but despite the achievement, I had zero motivation to make music and didn't go into my basement for five months except to wash clothes. I even stopped digging for records, which was something I had done weekly since I was 10 years old. Finding inspiration was like finding a straight man who won't admit that he wants to bone the dog shit out of Sarah Palin.

A flood ravaged my basement that summer, but with the exception of trying to salvage my most valuable records in frenzy, my reaction to the mishap was disturbingly calm. I cleaned up the water solely to prevent mold and left the studio in shambles until it flooded again a year later. To this day, I can't pinpoint exactly why I completely lost interest in something that consumed who I was, nor can I explain it to people who wonder why the fuck I couldn't just go into the studio and make something. After ignoring the 800-pound gorilla riding shotgun in the Cadillac and becoming a full-time high school sports reporter barely getting by, I finally sought closure.

A moment of clarity

Recently, Fat Beats gave me the option of taking back my thousands of unsold CDs and records or having them destroyed at a recycling plant. The returns were piling up in the warehouse and, according to them, my music hadn't been ordered in years. Neither of us had enough room for the pallets of leftover product. Destroying my shit was comparable to pulling a relative off life support, but it also symbolized something that had to be done in order to completely move forward and lock the gate behind me. I gave them permission to turn on the melting machines for closure's sake. Two days later, my digital distributor informed me (via Certified Mail) that they were dropping me from their roster for poor sales. I was in the left lane of the Bitter Old Man Expressway and repudiated all things J-Zone until I learned two of life's most important lessons while half-watching one of those crash and burn VH1 *Behind the Music* documentaries: If you can't laugh at failure, you're dead in this world. If you can't find closure, you're buried alive and can never start over.

I took a $30 Red Lobster gift card that I had gotten for Christmas and cruised down the road for a ghetto seafood party. Once seated, I celebrated failure and closure over a plate of lobster and wood-fire grilled shrimp. I sat alone in the booth stuffing my face, wielding my knife and fork, and adjusting the bib that I had tucked into my shirt collar like a little kid. Suddenly I stopped, wiped my mouth on the bib, and broke out laughing uncontrollably.

Looking back on my days of cussing a bitch out with the lyrics from the No Face tape, engineering sessions for locals at Vee-Dubbs, cutting out cassette j-cards for my first album on the highway, and digging for records with my pops, I realize that those simple musical memories made me the happiest. Once your hobby and passion become your primary income, you can say you've "made it", but there's a catch - it's no longer just about doing whatever the fuck you want.

In reality, J-Zone in the music biz was a Kia Soul at the Player's Ball - a spunky little truck in its own way, but wildly out of place for the Pimp of the Year competition. Music has returned to being a hobby and occasional outlet for me. I can dig it. No regrets.

16. SUPERHEROES & PEERS

In 2011, there are more rappers, DJs, producers, label owners, promoters, interns, managers, and rap fellatio specialists than there are fans. Your average rap personality is a slob. Why can't we have more rap dietitians? Fans are in such short supply and great demand these days, that I'm willing to sidestep my 15-year stint in the game to chill with the bench warmers and be 90 percent fan, 10 percent artist.

My greatest achievements would be a toss-up between touching down in 14 different countries to do something I enjoyed and having a chance to cross paths and work with the superheroes of my adolescence. Whether it was giving a high-out-of-his-skull Redman the name of a Bill Cosby sample over the phone, getting an apology from MF Doom when he blew up my bathroom, receiving tips on longevity from Too $hort, chopping it up with Audio 2's Milk Dee about the making of *I Don't Care - The Album*, or watching Pete Rock bug out over the copy of Kool & the Gang's *Music Is The Message* on 8-track tape that I had in my basement, brushes with folks I grew up admiring made every bad day I endured in this business worth it. I wouldn't trade those experiences for a 1978 Cadillac Brougham. Certain folks in particular made my journey something to remember - my hat is tipped.

The Super 6

Biz Markie

As a court jester of rap, a spokesman for unattractive brothers, and a guy who sampled whatever the fuck he felt like sampling with a completely reckless and feigned ignorance of copyright law, my operation owes a lot to Biz. Therefore, when my first major outside production credit wound up on Biz's *Weekend Warrior* album in 2003, I had officially "made it" in my own mind. Over a decade after memorizing the lyrics to "The Dragon" and singing them to the stank breath kid in my seventh grade science class, I was driving down to Biz's Maryland recording studio to track our song, "Chinese Food."

"Yo man, I thought you'd be Chinese!" was the first thing the Diabolical Biz ever said to me - the beat I gave him for the song had an Asian-tinged sample. After he autographed my copy of the *Biz Never Sleeps* album and we tracked the beat, Biz spent an hour playing me DAT tapes of utterly insane Biz Mark shit that never saw the light of day. I still say if his record label put those songs on the album, *Weekend Warrior* wouldn't have flopped. To their credit, they did make "Chinese Food" the second single for the album (and the song he did with P-Diddy the B-side to it, which I still gloat about today), but that flopped too. Industry Rule #4081: J-Zone makes good music, but his appearance on your record doesn't help sales.

SUGA FREE

I get strange facial expressions from people when I boldly proclaim that Suga Free is the greatest artist to debut in the last 15 years. I truly feel that the man's music is pure unadulterated genius. The absorption of his *Street Gospel* album and the making of *Music for Tu Madre* were wholly responsible for me getting over my first hoodrat heartbreak in 1998. "I'd Rather Give You My Bitch" is lyrically my favorite rap song of all time and thanks to my man Med out in Cali, I got to see first-hand that Suga Free is as outrageously entertaining and pimpish in person as he is on record.

I flew out to Los Angeles to do an in-store at Tha Formula, a small graffiti paraphernalia and record shop. Med told me that he had contacted Suga Free's people and arranged to have him show up at the store to discuss us working together. I had a blank check and a beat CD in my back pocket, ready to make a pitch to the only rapper I would pay beyond my budget to have on *A Job Ain't Nuthin' but Work*, which I was in the midst of recording.

Two hours after his scheduled arrival, one of the only actual pimps in the rap game showed up. Apparently, the TVs in his car had drained the battery and he needed a jump, or so I was told. After a brief introduction and a handshake, I shuffled nervously through my beat CD in front of Suga and handful of spectators. He was the only artist I've ever been scared to play beats for. After all, he made classics with DJ Quik for years, so I was up against a seasoned and spoiled ear. Before I could glance at him for a facial reaction, he just let loose in a high-pitched west coast drawl:

"Oooooooh...yeah. Yes. Oh yes. I'll talk reeeeeaaaal bad about a bitch over sum'n like this."

He was brain damage serious. I looked at the in-store attendees' faces. We were all struggling with the same restraint. I excused myself, ran to the bathroom and fell into an uncontrollable fit of laughter for about two minutes. Suga Free was ready and willing to hop on my album as a guest; that in itself was one of my greatest musical triumphs. Things never materialized, but I never quit being a fan. Truth be told, I would've paid the pimp a clearance fee just to talk about talkin' bad about a bitch over my beat for 30 seconds.

Large Professor

After an hour discussing music with Large, I forgave him for lying to me about the SP-1200 when I was a green teenager. I've never encountered anyone who was more about the music itself than Large. Whether it was going digging for records, taking apart studio equipment, pulling out instruments for an out-of-nowhere impromptu funk band jam session, or riding a mountain bike 40 round trip miles in the summer heat to watch DJ sets at the Brooklyn Hip-Hop festival, Large is by far the most no-frills cat I've encountered on my journey. I respect that brother to the utmost for enduring the ups and downs of a shitty business while retaining his vibe. That's something that I and countless others haven't been able to do.

Hollywood Impact

Hollywood is a producer who never gets mentioned amongst some of hip-hop's greats and it's a damn shame. His work on niche market albums by Twin Hype, King Sun, and Style in the early '90s was pound for pound as good as anyone's production at the time. Hollywood's music had the uncanny distinction of sounding as unhinged as a Public Enemy record, but as dance floor-friendly as a *Club MTV* smash. I had the chance to meet Hollywood in 2003 through T.O.N.E (formerly Tony Tone from Style); he was the only producer I've ever had a listening session with where we both left talking about re-inventing the wheel. I played him *Sick of Bein' Rich*, he played me some unreleased beats, and there were at least 20 hi-fives between us in that session.

Prince Paul

As two quirky and humor-based producer personalities, Paul and I clicked immediately. One particular phone conversation with the producer of De La Soul and Handsome Boy Modeling School stood out as a defining moment.

When my career was on the decline in 2006, I was feverishly looking for new paths to reinvention. I even went the beat battle route, attempting to bring my comedic showmanship to events as devoid of personality as producer battles. That backfired as well. Although sucking whipped cream off foam titties in a Scion battle (where Paul and Pete Rock were judges) was fun and unique, I got the book thrown at me and walked off the stage to complete silence from a dumbfounded crowd. A conversation with Paul the morning after I stormed out of the Canal Room nightclub pissed off to the highest level of pisstivity and threw the foam titties into a trash heap on the sidewalk gave me a lot of insight.

"When I saw you up there struggling with that crowd, I saw myself," he told me via phone. As a fellow rule-breaker, Paul told me that there isn't much room for intricacies, subtle beat changes, and off the wall showmanship in the boom-bap world of beat battles; people in a crowded room just can't absorb it. The relevance of that theory went up tenfold when half of the other producers in the battle were low-calorie versions of Kanye West, Just Blaze, and J-Dilla. Paul shared stories from his career as a producer under RUSH Management, explaining how his whole approach was often misunderstood. As a longtime Prince Paul fan, his advice and shared anecdotes gave me the confidence to stay the course for a bit longer than I probably would have otherwise.

Cee-Lo

At the pinnacle of Gnarls Barkley's fame (their hit song, "Crazy", was working the pop charts with a remote control) Cee-Lo and Danger Mouse weren't too large to jump onto the tiny stage at NYC's CBGB night club the night it closed for good to perform my song "Disco Ho" with me. Even funnier was how I discovered that Cee-Lo liked that song.

"Man, Cee-Lo keeps singing "Disco Ho" on the tour bus," Mouse told me over the phone the day before my NYC retirement show. "I told him about your retirement show tomorrow, he wants to sing the chorus for you." I told him to stop bullshittin', there's no way that the artist on the biggest record in the world at the time knew anything about J-Zone. The Average Joe didn't know or care who J-Zone was; why would Cee-Lo?

"Hold on," Mouse told me. After some ruffling on the phone, the voice on the other end took on a countrified drawl:

"Nigga, these hooooooooeees wanna dance!"

I damn near shit on myself. Cee-Lo started talking about my catalog and broke down three or four of my albums in the same manner Just Blaze did when I met him. What baffled me was how the fuck people making platinum albums were fans of mine, but I had about 1,500 fans at that point. However, I was most shocked at Cee-Lo's pick for his favorite J-Zone album.

"Man, you and Dick $tallion with that *Gorilla Pimps* shit; that's the best shit you ever did!" he near screamed. I couldn't help but laugh at the drunken, ho-slapping, satirical, and never officially released comedy album that $tallion and I made in four hours being loved by a pop star. If you think I objected though, you're smoking something.

Witnessing Gnarls Barkley hop on stage to perform "Disco Ho" with me that night was one of the most memorable events of my journey. The performance stands today on YouTube as one of a miniscule number of videos featuring Cee-Lo that has under 20,000 views, but the memory itself trumps the validation. Gnarls was on top of the world and performing at Hollywood A-list events, but they spent their Wednesday night with a low-on-the-totem-pole rap artist in an incubator-sized club with 100 people on hand to see it. Not bad for a "failure." Cee-Lo is living proof that even mega-stars are music fans at the core. Most of them don't discriminate on the basis of sales and "success." It wouldn't surprise me if Eminem or Madonna were bumping some obscure artist their fans never heard of on their tour buses. That obscure artist is probably struggling to keep his or her lights on, but I've learned that sometimes shit just works that way and I've finally accepted being one of those artists. Special shout outs to all I've crossed paths with and the result was an enjoyable musical experience. Peace.

PArt TwO:
i SMELL BuLLShit!

17. BACK ON THE PLANTATION

"BitCh, get a Job." - Sadat X

I couldn't believe what I was hearing after the high school basketball game I had been covering was over.

"Yo man, you J-Zone?" the point guard asked me before I could ask him about his 19 point, 8 assist performance.

I asked him to repeat his question. Not to flatter myself, but to make sure I'd heard him correctly. My ears weren't bullshittin'.

"Ummm," I stammered.

"Dude," he cut me off. "The YouTube videos of you chillin' in the drive-thru at White Castle and licking whipped cream off those foam titties are classic!"

I was part shocked that someone born after 1985 knew who I was by face, part embarrassed that my attempts to be professional as a sports reporter were trumped by being known as the Onion Ring and Titty Man, and part flattered that an obscure and pseudo-famous rap guy like myself was even remembered years after my modest music career had gone kaput. I guess that's what happens to the quasi-successful middle ground rap man who's teetering the top of a fence that separates two universes - he eventually falls over to the "real" job side. And it fucks up folks who fail to realize he wasn't that famous in the first place.

LEVELS OF STATUS

First, we have the megastar. When the musical careers of 50 Cent, Lil' Wayne, and Kanye West come to a halt, there's an ice cube's chance under a fat girl's ass that they would ever work nine-to-five jobs. Imagine Wayne attempting to pass a piss test to become a second grade teacher and kissing Birdman on the mouth for good luck before taking the ATS-W exam. What about Kanye raking up $11 an hour to re-rack returned U.S. Polo Association shirts at Sears?

When the musical endeavors of megastars no longer hold any weight, they've already become big enough entities to make a living via movies, their own lines of wife-beater shirts, and unscheduled appearances at events where they break Moet bottles over the heads of artists who are hot at the moment for pay. They'd never dare step into a nine-to-five; it just doesn't compute after that much time on top. If you're naturally crazy or irresponsible enough to never stand a chance in the world of day jobs, God usually grants you success in entertainment so you won't starve to death.

Next, we have the Recreational Indie Rap Artist (RIRA). The Raptionary would define him as such:

Recreational Indie Rap Artist: *(reck-ree-ayshun-ul-indee-rap-ahrtist)* **noun.** 1. A rap hobbyist who earns his living outside of the music business. Thus, he can typically afford to release music and perform for free.

The pinnacle of his career was holding down the opening slot at shows and churning out an album that was a compilation of all his 12" singles and mixtape freestyles. After his post-soundcheck performance, the RIRA broke out immediately because he had to work in the morning. Chances that he'll ever be recognized in public long after he's active are hovering at around zero and he'll never have to field questions about why he never "made it" or why he's no longer giving enough of a shit to still be trying. Through it all, the RIRA avoids the culture shock of entering the nine-to-five world in his 30s and 40s. Thus, his predicament is better than one would think.

I can't forget about the "Golden Era" legends. Current releases from them are scarce, but they've laid enough hip-hop classics to wax to get placement in respected foreign music festivals or the *Rock the Bells* tour. Their aforementioned classic song catalogs also allow them to have their music licensed on a major scale and avoid getting laughed off the phone when they name their guest appearance fee.

But the most enigmatic of all is the quasi-successful middle ground musician. He got to enjoy his I-do-what-I-love-for-a-living phase, only to be awoken by a 500-foot drop into the working world that the other levels of entertainer don't typically experience. He had potential, but never really got over the hump. His music is now largely available for free on various blogs and virus-laden bit torrents on the internet, but these days he's got bigger fish to fry - like trying to get some overtime. By the time he gets home, he spends his hour of free time in the kitchen preparing tomorrow's bag lunch and ironing his shirt and slacks.

It can take anything from a drastic plunge in record sales, kids, impending financial instability, a growing disinterest in the music business, or the realization that paying for an MRI with no health insurance costs what that gold toilet in Master P's bathroom costs - any or all of the above can make the quasi-successful rap guy fall into this reality. This reality is now mine. I once trotted the globe, had the option of sleeping until noon, plugged women on different continents based on the perception that I was more famous than I really was, and landed on the cover of a skater magazine with a music article or two in it. In my current reality, those conquests hold as much weight as a copy of Bobby Seale's *Seize the Time* at a Tea Party meeting. In this reality, I'm starting from zero.

A JOB AIN'T NUTHIN' BUT WORK: BE CAREFUL WHAT YOU WISH FOR

In 2009, it was painfully clear that it was time for me to make some real loot. Teaching a music course at my Alma mater was gratifying, but short-lived thanks to state budget cuts. My mother suggested that I go back to school to become a K-12 teacher, but what kids will listen to some guy telling them to read pages 17-31 for homework after they go on YouTube and discover he made a song about accidentally taking an underage girl to the movies and treating her to a box of Sno-Caps? After two years of matching James Evans from Good Times' yearly salary via random DJ gigs and beat sales, sports reporting, fruitless job hunting, and blogging for charity, I finally got my first "real" job in over a decade.

I landed the job due to my being humble enough to know that there's no such thing as being "overqualified" these days. After Katie from Utah moves to NYC to live out her dream via an exorbitantly-priced Master's degree in education, you can find her teaching alright... teaching the new girl at the bar how to pour a Guinness Stout and use the right amount of grenadine in a Tequila Sunrise. Therefore, I didn't scoff at pushing gym memberships for my re-introduction to the working world. Eleven years after my small record label took flight and I told my boss at Automobile Club of America to go fuck himself, I was telling some wide and fried heifer she was a Milk Dud away from having a heart attack, and dropping $222 upfront and $36 a month was the only action that could prevent her caked-up arteries from slamming the breaks on her ticker.

"Look ma'am, you're in trouble if you don't lose weight," I pitched on my first sale attempt. "Can I tell you about our summer special?"

Hey, don't scowl at me. The only way to make any real money in America is via the next person's fear. Ask the church, your mechanic, your lawyer, your shrink, the IRS, the creators of match.com, your HMO, or Suge

Knight circa 1997. Fear-based income is recession-proof; I tried to get rich via making people fear fatness.

When you're pitching a gym membership to every person who comes through the door like they're a bitch with a fat ass and you just came home from Rikers, you tend to be pretty low on the respect meter in the eyes of snobs in Nouveau York. People 'round these parts would rather drink wine, eat expensive cheeses, collect degrees like Garbage Pail Kid cards, and give you that bourgeois impression that they're doing something significant when they're doggy paddling in school debt. There are no real "qualifications" for sales jobs at gyms, so a dinner conversation with your girlfriend's family feels something like a pleather turtle neck. To chat it up with some of the gym's members about the life and times of "The Situation" from *Jersey Shore* can be a bit taxing too. It's also worth noting that in an industry where many men have gone bald from pumping steroids, I was known as "the guy with the hair."

"Jay, you can't let potential members walk out the door," my boss pounded daily throughout my first month on the job. "They can say they can't afford the gym or 'I'll think about it' all they want. If they walk out, you lost."

I lost quite a bit. I did find moderate success tracking down due fees from members over the phone, but that prowess can be attributed to a decade of chasing dollar store rap moguls around for the remaining $4.50 owed on a $500 beat they bought from me. Nonetheless, when it came to meeting my sales quota and stacking that commission, I was a blown transmission. My last day on the job featured me angrily attacking the gumball machines at the front of the gym for no valid reason whatsoever. I realized then that I was in no shape to be working in the real world.

To be fair, there were some very real and sharp people at the gym. The experience gave me a take on some other folks besides hip-hop brats. One day I fell into a discussion with a woman who had spent some time in Europe. When I began to give accounts of my time spent overseas as a little-known musician, she asked me if I attended college. After all, how could a thirty-something year old black man with a nappy 'fro and honey oat bread Subway sandwich crumbs on his gym staff shirt be educated and well-traveled enough to know anything about Iceland? The vibe only got more bizarre when she learned I graduated college with honors. Then, the elephant Crip-walked through the gym's doors and farted.

"Jay," she said flatly. "You're a little overqualified to be working at a gym."

No. "Overqualified" is a fancy synonym for "yeah, whatever nigga, just grab a broom." The Raptionary would define a music degree like this:

Music Degree: *(myoo-zik dih-gree)* **noun.**

1. A laminated document from a university that is primarily used as a dustpan. It comes in handy when sweeping up paper shreds, pushpins, and random shit off the office floor.

When the gym's basement flooded, that "overqualified" shit gave me an insane amount of leverage over the rest of the staff - I got to use the squeegee instead of the mop. Jobs in the working world share one parallel with the entertainment business - both are based on timing and who you know. A lot of people with music business connections don't have many working world connections. That meant that I was the perfect candidate to change the gym's TV channel when that whale-sized, party plate-ordering broad on the recumbent bike just had to watch the God damn Food Network when everyone else wanted World Cup soccer. I may have been the only person on the gym staff with a Bachelor's degree, but the only piece of paper worth diddly shit in my reality was the sales sheet. Decade-old college achievements didn't produce numbers. My ability to convince Big Shirley to stop eating mofongo and buy a personal training package did. That lucrative skill is typically learned sometime around high school, when you're competing with drug dealers and jocks to pull girls. It's called the gift of gab, and if you're attempting to hurdle-hop in the real world without it, you're fucked. Take your 30-page senior thesis and shove it up your ass.

Working in sales also made me more curmudgeonly than I already was, because constant smiling is a requisite.

"Jay, c'mon bro," my boss would plead. "You need to smile more!"

My theory on smiling unnecessarily goes like this: Would you stand at the urinal if you didn't have to take a leak? Would you just pull your cock out, stand there holding it, and gaze starry-eyed at the Koehler logo on the top of the urinal simply because you have the ability to shoot piss from it? Case closed. I was without a doubt the Homie D. Clown of the fitness industry for four months.

I even snatched up a side job to supplement my gym income. When I discovered that the man in charge at the side job was an ex-convict, I appraised the value of an Arts Degree in America. Then, I thought of Katie with that bad ass 40K Master's degree and pouring that Guinness Stout like a fuckin' champ. Now, are we still going to sit up here and say an overpriced education is the way and crime doesn't pay? Right, and Robin Givens married Mike Tyson for his extensive vocabulary.

119

CRUNCHING NUMBERS

Today, I'm juggling a temporary support staff job in a financially-strapped school district and three low-paying side jobs. At school, the kids keep me sharp by testing my wits daily. (When my ex-barber zeeked my afro and turned it into an accidental hi-top fade, the kids gave me my current nickname around school: "House Party"). My fellow staff members are chill enough to make work bearable, enjoyable even. (The principal breaks into the Kid-N-Play kick step dance whenever I enter his office.) My supervisor is a human encyclopedia and the greatest boss I've ever had. It's also worth noting that he was Rakim's sixth grade math teacher. Soaking up daily spills of knowledge from the man who taught arguably the greatest MC of all time how to put seven MCs in a line and mathematically destroy 'em makes my days that much greater. However, policy says I'm not entitled to full salary and benefits for doing a job that I've even been told I'm "overqualified" for (yet the person I replaced got full salary and benefits) because I didn't take a test that isn't even being offered for another two years. Yeah, that makes as much sense as the girl with the Coke bottle body getting the record deal over the fat girl with the golden voice, but that's just the way shit goes. The rulebook protocol of nine-to-fives and the dysfunctional protocol of the music business - neither is better than the other. Just pick your poison and develop and immunity to it.

Some of my music peers have been cornered into doing arbitrary freelance work and shooting social network pleas for relevance. Financially, the music world has become a barren wasteland for many, so some days it seems like squaring up for a 30-year bid in the world of "mature adults" is the move. After a ten month lease in that world, I can't endorse it. I don't even know if I can fully fault washed-up rappers for not growing up and moving on, because most of them wouldn't last a nanosecond over here anyway. When you got a record deal in 1991 at age 19 and have never played a pawn in the working world, snapping into it at age 39 is a heroin withdrawal.

The average adult equates drab conformity with maturity and stability. Yeah, that's the spirit! Get acclimated with your Jon Arbuckle-esque, boring-ass life and inspire others to do the same, because "it's time." Never ruffle feathers by challenging protocol that hinders your progress, sporting radical haircuts as an adult, or standing up (or down) to your midget boss when he enters the room to throw his (lack of) height around. Those are a few of the requisites of "getting your grown man on". Putting up with bullshit is acceptable because the bills keep coming and nobody else you know can even find a job. We all do what we must to survive, but save the Baby Boomer rhetoric about taking pride in jobs that don't take pride in us. I can hear these Creflo Dollar-followin', T.D. Jakes-readin', chitterling-eatin', Steve Harvey suit-wearin', "We Shall Overcome" singin' fools in my neighborhood giving me the riot act now.

"You need to get you a good job," they'll advise me in diction reminis-cent of a bumbling slave in a 1940s flick. "One of them city jobs like Cousin Jimmy had. Cousin Jimmy was light-skinnded like you, he could have passed. If you cut all that damn nappy ass hair off your head, you could pass too. You also need Jesus in your life. Yeah, then one day you can be the bigger house boss and retire down south! That's what I fittin' to do, get my pension! Now, pass that Kool-Aid and fry up that chicken, boy!"

Negro please. Go audition for *Meet the Browns* or something. You can't joke about the man working at Burger King anymore; he makes the same money as the muthafucka in the cubicle dressed "business casual" who does no business and casually answers phones. And as for Jesus, I saw him in front of the Laundromat last week. He asked to borrow a quarter and a Snuggle sheet so he could finish drying his robe.

"Well, what about your 401k and your pension?" asks the pedestrian American. Ah, your 401k, right, that beloved three-digit number. Y'all want to talk numbers, eh? Sure, let's crunch some.

Your retirement money usually kicks in at around 67 years of age. I'm currently 34 years of age and still haven't found my lifetime gig, which means I'll be working until I'm about 79 years of age if I want to "retire". Roughly 25 percent of my check goes to taxes. I spend $55 a week in gas to commute 50 round trip miles a day to work because my 2001 Volkswagen Passat with the V6 engine only behaves on 89 or 93 octane gas that currently pumps at about $4.23 and $4.39 a gallon, respectively. Most jobs I've been "eligible" for with my rap resume offer 0 benefits, so I'm spending $500 a month for health insurance so I don't have to pay a $25,000 hospital bill if I tear my ACL play-ing a pick-up game of 21. I've been told the key to making more money in America is to spend $40,000 to attain a Master's degree. Right, then I'll make $37,000 a year instead of $21,000. My school debt will consequently lower my credit score to about 590, before I get laid off and am back to making $8 an hour working at a 7-11. Those IRAs I purchased in my 20s look like pussy in a glass vase on the other side of the bars to a convict doing 15 to 25, but I'll get penalized 35 percent if I touch them before I turn 61. I've spent 10 months as a working stiff and can damn near qualify for Section 8. Meanwhile, Snooki just made $32,000 to speak at Rutgers University based on 2 tits, a 97 percent UV tan, and 1/3 of a brain. The sum of all that arithmetic is not a number but a statement: In 2011, it pays to be a psycho. If that plan backfires, you still won't be any worse off than Katie, our 40K educated, beer-pouring quasi-educator.

The job doesn't want to provide benefits, but if the barbershop gets shot up while you're sitting in the chair getting your "presentable" and "grown" haircut for work, who pays your medical bills?

"Now Jay, don't be rash," a friend once told me after he had obviously taken his nose to Peru and had a party. "Behave and be cautious in the workplace because your future is at stake."

I guess that means I can't show up to work wearing a clip-on tie with Master P's face on it because I may get written up for insubordination. I don't want that, because with $12 an hour and century-old, rigid company policy dangling over my head and leaking bullshit like a busted piñata, a world of opportunity is truly on the horizon. One day I may get a shot at becoming the boss, so I'd better behave! You're right man, I'll be more careful when choosing my wardrobe, hairstyle, and facial expressions.

Nigga please. While I'm being plucked out of a job due to bureaucracy and being told to go buy a Ph.D., some bird-brained broad has cooned her way into a top-paying gig on *Basketball Wives* after some ball player skeeted in her face and bought her a Ford Focus afterward. Want me to get a "presentable" haircut for work? Present me a salary I can survive on, cunt mouth.

If you were somehow able to sustain your career in entertainment and never had to punch a clock in your adult life, I sincerely hope you never will. But what if you have a family that depends on every plantation-fed nickel that trickles into your overdrawn bank account and your entertainment career is over? Well, you better take a ride to Runnemede, New Jersey, visit Mister Softee headquarters and cop yourself an ice cream truck that sits on some 25" rims. Start slangin' Snow Cones my brother, because he who follows the rules in America today will almost always lose.

18. GO GO GADGET HO!

I need a land line bitch. It's only right; cell phones are throwing a 140 mph fastball at mankind. My recent field trips into the technology-driven jungle of night life have caused my sex drive to wane to the point that my hand is more enticing than being in the presence of a new and steadily growing breed of woman:

The Gadget Ho
Despite the examples given, Gadget Hoes can be male or female.

Some Gadget Hoes prefer Androids, some prefer Blackberries, and some prefer iPhones, but a Gadget Ho is a Gadget Ho, no matter the weapon. In simpler terms, a Gadget Ho is a cell phone slut.

Long before Gadget Hoes roamed the Earth (and us cavemen spiked drinks and mingled with sloppy drunk broads as protocol), man's main nemesis in the pursuit of a woman had a heartbeat. She didn't require a charger, but she had a battery in her back that was juiced by a pack of undesirable scallywags. She was none other than the infamous Huddle Ho. You remember the Huddle Ho, don't you? She met you, she talked to you, she liked you, but she never left with you. Why? She had a huddle with her three wide and fried friends in the ladies room, where they told her how she could do much better and you weren't worth her number. They were on the verge of going home alone, so they put a cease and desist on your pound party to make us all equally miserable. After the restroom huddle, the Huddle Ho came back with her buffalo trio in tow and the vibe was never the same. You were with your hand that night simply because those lousy, sloth broads decided that your time was up. Men got hip and began to combat that with some offensive strategy, implementing three of their own friends to occupy the Huddle Ho's cockblocker brigade. Those were the quality days of old, when the involvement of humans leveled the playing field. Unfortunately, man can't trump technology; the Gadget Ho is sending the Huddle Ho the way of the pterodactyl. Picture this:

The music is blaring, people are congregating in small pockets of the club, a handful are even dancing. Not the Gadget Ho. She finds a small cranny of the club to bury herself with her Asthma pump (read: cell phone) and engage in who knows what. As Cyber-Hussy sets the stages for early carpal tunnel onset, texting away with a marshmallow-eating grin on her face, I'm forced to wonder what she's writing and receiving that's so fuckin' amusing that she just can't engulf herself in it in the comfort of her own home, on a park bench, or in a shit-infested Porta-Potty on the Vans Warped Tour. Is it a stock tip from Randolph & Mortimer on the next frozen orange crop? Did T-Mobile get a street date for *Detox* from Dr. Dre himself? Or is it simply a seminar in the lingo that only people born post-1990 can fully understand? You know, LMFAO, SMH, ROTFL, OMG, IDK, and FML, among other odorless brain farts.

The Gadget Ho unfortunately is a victim of her own lifestyle when attempting to breast-stroke in the river of actual human interaction. I discovered this when I began to chat up a cute 27-year-old broad worth a 12 minute episode at an NYC lounge. I wasn't expecting much intellect from the tramp when she was telling me a story about her move to NYC from Wyoming, but then the spokes fell completely off the Cadillac hub cap.

"It was hilarious, I was ROTFL," she said in a deadpan tone and sporting a still grill. The whole exchange had the same effect on my sex drive as the thought of Rosanne Barr butt naked eating a gyro on my living room sofa would. C'mon bitch, did you not want to roll on the floor and laugh, so you gave me text shorthand? I probably would've earned a stripe on the uniform had I possessed the patience; I opted to go home and watch *Hogan's Heroes* for the remainder of the night. Yes, I've gotten that shallow and impatient in my old age. If I wanna smash a robot, I've got Rosie from *The Jetsons* on speed dial. If you really get the urge to roll on the floor and laugh, just do it you dumb broad.

I often recall the days of pay phone pimpin, when $0.25 gave you a few minutes to convince a girl to come outside. Additionally, one of those minutes was lost if her parent answered the phone and stalled you. That meant your rap had to be fierce, because you were fresh out of pocket change and thus couldn't extend the talk time; you got right to the point. Nowadays, I'm receiving a bunch of LOLs, "winks", and smiley faces from some cheese bus bimbo who's well into her 30s. I guess the "wink" means I can just come right on over and place my nuts on your forehead, right? It doesn't? Well Gadget Ho, 86 the fuckin' emoticons, pick up the God damn phone and tell me what the fuck you're trying to say. Otherwise, I waste three hours doing back and forth texting just to find out you want to put me in the Friend Zone.

It seems as if every thought and statement now has a 140-character limit, regardless of whether it's spoken or written. If you don't have to speak or write in complete sentences to maneuver your way through the day, you eventually become as inept as the Wyoming Wench was. She offered me her seven digits (real OGs still say "seven digits"; if you say "ten digits", you're a fuckin' fruitcake), but a Gadget Ho encounter destroyed my social gumption for the night.

The Gadget Ho has even jumped on the fitness bandwagon, joining gyms with monthly fees that can reach $100. She must get a kick out of hopping on the treadmill to send text messages throughout her entire workout, because she can easily punch in an "LOL" or two when the God damn treadmill is only on level 2. That would explain why her text messaging package has increased each year, but she's a bigger piece of streak-o-lean than she was when she first joined the gym in 2002.

Gadget Hoes and the Holidays

When the holiday season is in full swing, you know what that means. My enemy is in full attack mode. No, not the long lines in Wal-Mart, Black Friday, or milquetoast Christmas Music (somebody play the Death Row Christmas album for once), but holiday-related mass text messages from the Gadget Ho. The Trifling Triumvirate of Thanksgiving, Christmas, and New Years never fail to provide you with proof of which Gadget Hoes really shouldn't have your phone number.

First off, anybody who takes one specific day to acknowledge or do something is a little queer in my book. There are 365 days in a year. If you're only thankful, giving, or adhering to a resolution on one of those days, you need help. I don't celebrate anything because I'm ornery most of the time, but when I want to give thanks, give a gift, or set a goal; I'm not looking at the calendar.

Additionally, having somebody's phone number is a privilege, a sign of respect. Don't assume that they have unlimited texting in their phone plan. They shouldn't have to sign up for it because you want to save time when doling out arbitrary greetings, either. I'm sick of getting texts like these:

- *Happy Turkey Day all!!!!*
    I only eat turkey on odd-numbered Mondays in July.

- *Merry Christmas everybody!!*
    I don't celebrate Christmas, I celebrate Groundhog Day.

127

- May you all prosper and reach your goals and resolutions in 2011!!

Where was this good will in June of 2009 when I needed it? Why do I have to wait until New Years to get a $0.15 good luck charm from you? Better yet, if you want to start going to the gym to lose some weight, why not go in October and stop ordering the God damn party plate today?

Every year around November 21st, I inform everybody of my disgust with these mass text messages so history doesn't repeat itself. After getting a $24 and $14 bill for texts alone in December 2008 and December 2007, respectively, I was cornered into getting a 400 free text a month plan to save some money. These days, I'm typically closing in on my 400 free texts around December 2nd, when the cycle's end is 17 days away. Between Thanksgiving and New Years, I watch my 400 texts dwindle down the drain via disingenuous greetings, many from people who got my number from some other rap personality without my permission. If you ask me for my number and I look at you funny, I'm sizing you up to see if you're the type to send mass texts. If I give you my e-mail instead, you know what time it is. I anticipate going over my 400 text limit by about 47 texts in December and I get charged the standard $0.15 a text when I pass 400. Let's do some arithmetic:

47 Text Messages @ $0.15 each = $7.05

About half of these texts are from people whose numbers aren't saved in my phone, so I have to call them back to see who they are and cuss them out. About 90 percent go to that robot voicemail message in which the bitch only tells you "222-403-0712 is not available" because the culprit is scared to put a personal greeting on the outgoing message. Then they text me again while I'm leaving a voicemail, like "What's up?" What the fuck do you mean, "What's up?" Pick up the God damn phone, dick mouth.

That's an additional $0.15.

Most of these texts are during peak hours, so I get charged for approximately 22 one minute calls before 9PM trying to get reimbursed my 15 cents via phone call. I have 600 anytime and free nights and weekends on my plan. I usually use about 587 minutes in the winter months because I like to leave some room and not get charged $1.25 per minute for going over 600. Therefore, I run a risk of going over my anytime minutes by approximately 5 minutes.

$$5 \ minutes \ @ \ \$1.25 \ per \ minute = \$6.25$$

Taxes and fees for the aforementioned activity are about $1.75

$$\$7.05 + \$0.15 + \$6.25 + \$1.75 = \$15.20$$

That's $15.20 spent for no reason at all. I've been victimized for having a cell phone and Gadget Hoes having my number. Texts pile up like L blocks in a game of *Tetris* when Christmas rolls around, and if I up my plan, that's another $10 per month and $120 for the year. At the end of it all, that's $140 including taxes and surcharges. I can hear y'all talkin' shit about me right now.

Yo man, Zone is mad cheap. He's pitchin' a bitch over $15.

Yes. I'm very cheap, but peep this: If you walked into White Castle and the cashier asked you for $15.20, but you didn't ask to buy any food, would you just give it to him simply because you were in there? What about if you go to CVS and you want $15.20 worth of vitamins? Every human being should have vitamins, but your $15.20 went towards something that you received against your will. Can you still get those vitamins without the $15.20?

People who don't abuse their phones are beaten into purchasing unnecessary features these days. That's like owning an iPod and being forced to buy Jewel's latest album on iTunes because 70 percent of the world bought her shit. Let that marinate for a second. In the meantime, here is a list of things I can do with $15.20:

- Get a shape-up and have some bread left over for a new toothbrush, one of the good ones with the bristles that reach deep into the gums and massage them.

- Fill 1/3 my tank with Mobil 89 Premium gas

- Cop a 6 pack of Adidas athletic crew socks at Marshall's and still have money left over to buy a newspaper.

- Order the Fat Boys' *Disorderlies* and Dolemite's *Avenging Disco Godfather* on DVD (including shipping) at Amazon.

Every holiday season, I send my mission statement out to the Gadget Hoes early, hoping to thwart some of this crap. But I swear on a stack of James Brown 45s, I'm sending out invoices from the publish date of this book forward for any Gadget Ho behavior that shows up on my phone bill. Try me if you think I'm bullshittin'.

The Cousins Of the Gadget HO: FLash HO and Cosmo HO

Camera phones and digital cameras have also taken over nightlife. This leads me to the cousins of the Gadget Ho: the Flash Ho and the Cosmo Ho.

Bitch, I know you just joined Facebook and you just hate that picture of yourself you were tagged in because you were caught off guard. Now you want to get the ever so clever shot of you and your raggedy, salmonella bird-ass friends all together holding your $15 Cosmos.

"OMG!! We're all here, this is awesome, let's take a picture!" the Flash Ho will scream. First, she'll summon the bird patrol (who are all holding their Cosmo glasses with the little umbrellas in them) to meet her in a corner of the club. It's only right; the Flash Ho is the ringleader of the Cosmo Ho gang. When all of the Cosmo Hoes are all present and accounted for, Flash Ho will look my way. "Excuse me, can you take a picture for us?"

If I tell the Flash Ho that I want my knob buffed in exchange, am I wrong? Quid pro quo, ho, my name ain't Hiro. The first time I was asked to do that, I obliged. I figured maybe it would open up conversation with the Flash Ho or one of the Cosmo Hoes, but the Ho harem left shortly after. Their sole purpose for coming to a lounge with a $5 cover was to have a few wall photos. Of course the other Cosmo Hoes in the picture would all comment on Twitter, MySpace, Google Plus, Yelp, and Facebook about how good the others look, but how they themselves look so fat, "LOL." Oh yeah, Facebook. Let's talk about that.

a gadget ho encounter

19. THE GROWN FOLKS' PLAYGROUND

At first, it was cool.

There's nothing like catching up with friends and acquaintances from years past. Then there's the luxury of having everybody from your grade school cronies to the current girl you're trying to stain the sheets of all in one place. You can chronicle your boring day for everyone and do the little bullshit quizzes with the spelling errors in the questions. Great.

If I had to choose though, I'd say Facebook's greatest asset is the gratification of payback via cyberspace reunion. That means seeing the fly girl from high school who predicted to your face that you'd wind up like one of those kids that Joe Clark called onto the stage and "expurgated" at the beginning of *Lean on Me.* In 2011, she looks like she struck an all-you-can-eat endorsement deal with Entenmann's. She also married some aspiring party promoter with seven teeth. I love to see shit like that. Facebook is nothing but a harmless little egomaniacal game of *Outburst* for all age groups. Or is it really that innocuous?

Unfortunately (like all things new, hip, and addictive), there's a dark side. Do you remember MySpace? Yeah, it took me a second to remember too, but at least that site had the nifty little approve comment feature. If somebody was going to remind you that you lost your virginity to someone with a Jheri curl, it was your choice to approve it. Facebook hasn't made those strides, so adding somebody you don't really know or haven't spoken to in years as a friend can be major trouble. Only my close friends can get on my page and post about me having occasional mean outbreaks of dandruff, and that's why I always wear light colored shirts when I get around the broads. Plus, responding to anything at all can get you in some Steve McGarrett vs. Wo Fat-level beef if a non-mutual friend of the person you're responding to feels the need to cyber-thug with a personal attack.

Let's not neglect that landmine of relationship status changes, and the fact that an ugly break up will put you in a Catch 22. Why? If you delete your ex, they PMS on you. If you leave him or her in your friends, you have to worry about something slick appearing on your page when you're not home.

Facebook knows that users need to keep an eye on their pages 24/7, in case some clown feels the urge to be The Ethernet Gangsta and the rest of your friends see it. Therefore, everybody now needs Facebook for Mobile to police their pages. Ch-ching!

dislike

I've gone through one too many 'what the fuck?' reactions to shit posted on my wall and consequently disabled it to chorus of "why the fuck can't I write on your wall?" complaints. Any information you want me to know can be sent via e-mail. Any information you want people to know about me can be delivered by e-mailing all 412 of my friends directly. That's a small task if you think it's so crucial that they all know about my dandruff problem. Here are the Six Deadly Sins in The Grown Folks' Playground:

1. ReLationship crap

If seeing your ex's updates appear on your news feed or their picture randomly come up on your front page makes your heart drop, drop 'em. Closure is golden and so underrated. Even though you're through, the ex is going to get nosy, snoop around your page to see something he or she doesn't like, and react like you're still an item. In disgust, they'll type something. Before you know it, you have your friends calling you in the street saying, "Yo, some girl named Denise just wrote on your wall that you drool when you eat cereal." Now that shit is up there until you can get to a computer to delete it if you don't have Facebook for Mobile. Furthermore, the new girl you're diggin' is afraid to take up your offer to come to the crib for some Cap'n Crunch because she saw the shit. This is corny. If you're an adult, listen and listen well.

> *What happens between you and your significant other is your business; nobody gives a shit.*

And Jesus, the change of relationship status shit. When it happens, you can bet your last roll of toilet paper while stranded on the bowl that people will comment on this. Ladies, you'll get plenty of stupid parenthesis and semi-colon combinations that are supposed to symbolize sad faces. Fellas, you'll get a lot of "you can do better" comments from broads who never gave you any pussy anyway (and never will) because they're your "friends" and they prefer being treated like a door-to-door Jehovah's Witness by their boyfriends.

Many make the dire mistake of not removing the change of relationship status from the news feed. Leaving it up is a Grade 'A' no-no, which is why I've gotten into arguments with girls I've dated about my staunch refusal to even put my relationship status on my page. If we don't end up married, the status will only be more of a headache when we go our separate ways. If we do get married and eventually split, it's just another formality in our divorce settlement.

"Are you embarrassed to let people know we're an item?" your partner will ask you at a very awkward moment when you're wolfing down some chicken tikka on a date. "Or are you trying to insinuate that you're not taken so you can approach other women on Facebook?"

This is how you respond: "People in the 1970s had relationships without Facebook relationship statuses and did just fine, you'll get over it."

2. Debates and Responses to Posted Items and Statuses

I love a heated debate. Even if it involves people I don't know. But keep in mind, throwing personal attacks at people you don't know makes you look like a fuck head.

Awhile back, my man posted a status update about parents assuming more responsibility for naming their kids. Specifically, it was about the choices of names we see in the black community, and if they affect the kids as they venture into adulthood. After all, naming your daughter Bonequeesha is not acceptable. I must say, the topic appealed to me. I'm Black, I live a black community, and I work in a school district that's 77 percent black, so I put my two cents in. My man made a joke about one of the made up names and I responded with a "haha." All of a sudden, one of his friends was berating me in the third person. Why? She assumed I was white and being insensitive. The fact that I'm a light-skinned black guy and people generally can't tell what the hell I am anyway is beside the point. Maybe she just assumed that because I wasn't Akon's complexion or wearing a Rocawear shirt, I must have been a racially-insensitive redneck. When I responded with some real facts about the topic at hand, that loudmouth bitch mysteriously went mute.

Facebook is an excellent soap box for gibberish, because nobody worth a half-bitten and drooled on York Peppermint Pattie is going to listen to the opinions of some ignorant, raggedy, cunt mouth broad in the real world. I used to watch *Jerry Springer* and wonder where the fuck they found those people. Now I know of three places where folks on that level of stupidity congregate - YouTube, Yahoo! Answers, and in your friends' non-mutual friends on Facebook. If you can't have an intelligent discussion without getting your drawers all cramped up in your ass, you're better off adding *Farmville*, *Mafia Wars*, or one of those other Facebook ho games.

3. COUPLE ACCOUNTS

No. Marriage and relationships can be swell, but don't forget that you're still an individual. Therefore, couples that go the route of making a Facebook page for themselves as a couple (ex. Rachel and David Jones' Facebook) need to be tossed into a vat of Burger King grease. Fellas, come on. If you allow your woman to talk you into believing that shit is cute, her dick is bigger than yours. Ladies, if your man is so whipped that he'd convince you to be joined at the hip online, you're one weak bitch. It only gets worse when every picture that isn't of them as a couple is of some meal they cooked as a couple that usually has bruschetta or some homemade chipotle lime sauce somewhere in it. That shit is oh so soft.

If the couple has children, there are the obligatory 400 pictures of their newborn, bowling ball-headed, slobbering, drooling machine. Kids are nifty, but how many pictures can you have of that brat? Infants are boring to look at, one picture will suffice. Of course all 400 pictures have an "awwww, he's adorable" caption underneath them, usually from the same stove-built bitch who is friends with the wife and living vicariously through this sappy-ass couple. Overly mature couples on Facebook deserve to be drubbed.

4. POINTLESS POSTING

The moment I saw "LOL" as somebody's status update, I knew we were in trouble. "LOL"? "LOL" what? What the fuck are you trying to say? If you want attention, run into KFC butt ass naked and tell the manager you're there to shoot dice with Colonel Sanders. Otherwise, if you don't have something witty, funny, deep, informative, or truthful to say, just shut the fuck up. The person who updated their status with the "LOL" was deleted immediately. Sounds petty of me, right? No. Do I need to be connected to an attention hungry adult who does shit like this just to stay on people's minds? No. Go get a Twitter account instead, and then die slowly behind a Chinese take-out joint somewhere.

5. Cyber-Threats From People From Your Past

Attempting to gauge who from your past is likely to be a lunatic today is a thorny process. A lot can happen to a muthafucka in 15 years, and there's really no way of knowing if someone has become a USDA choice basket case.

Donald was always a cool brother back in the day, and somewhat of a hero to me in high school. He was one half of a dope local rap group that put out an album, but even after the deal went south, we would trade records and chop it up for hours about music. He hooked up with a girl I was cool with from my high school, but they fell out. She got an order of protection against him and is preventing him from seeing his kid. I never saw Donald again, until he added me on Facebook 13 years later.

One month after it happened, I nearly choked on my fish sandwich when Donald posted a death threat on my wall for all 411 of my friends to see. A flurry of e-mails about what he was going to do to me for trying to fuck his girl back in '96 (which I never tried to do) came moments later. A 40-year-old man making threats via internet ranks pretty high on the enigmatic behavior list. I deleted and blocked Donald, but it made me wonder if I now had to monitor the behavior of my other 411 friends every minute of every day. After all, someone could choke on a chicken bone, get a flashback of when I threw a chicken nugget at them in the school cafeteria in 1990, and write "you're next" on my wall.

6. "POKing"

Do I really need to elaborate on this?

Look, I'm not trying to be Sgt. Killjoy here. I like to post videos, random thoughts, and articles that I think are funny, interesting, nostalgic or informative. It's even cool to reconnect with people, but realistically, how many of these people will you continue to correspond with after the initial, "It's been a long time, how have you been?!" Furthermore, how do you know what types of grudges, issues, and beefs these lunatics have acquired since you last saw them in January of 1991? Sometimes I wish you could just see all of a person's pictures without adding them, just to confirm that the girl who used to shit on you in 1992 is in fact a no tooth, slovenly, sloth whale of a broad these days. That way, you can rest assured without the awkwardness of a friend request and the disturbing silent activity that foreshadows a cyber-incident.

137

Since we're seemingly all in the eighth grade again, let's all get off Facebook fire drill-style and proceed back into the building to live our lives.

20. ANOTHER WASTED NIGHT

A night in the Life of a socially homeless man in New York City

New York City. The Rotten Granny Smith. Ol' Blue Eyes claimed that you want to be a part of it in his unmistakable tenor. Jay-Z found enough inspiration in this place to window dress it in a song that now finds a home in karaoke bars. New York Yankee hats are now being manufactured in pink, for fuck's sake. As a New York native, I'll claim this place until my ashes get tossed off the Throgs Neck Bridge, but I stumble off the road at the notion that NYC is some type of liberal melting pot. You know; a place where everyone intermingles and accepts those outside of their respective bubbles in some poster-worthy show of tolerance. A place where people wiggle in their seats with smile-coated IBS discomfort when discussing racism or class difference, although they cling to those differences for dear life when deciding which part of the social lunchroom to sit in.

An image of NYC's Union Square (where a diverse crowd cuts through the congested transportation hub to disperse back to their own respective enclaves) neatly captured in a magazine photo I saw once is as deceptive as a RuPaul photo; five percent of those people in the snapshot actually live there.

Brooklyn's long-standing racial tug-o-war (displayed in old Spike Lee films and Al Sharpton-quarterbacked rallies of the '80s) can seem like a blast from the past when walking through the northwestern quadrant of the borough today. A twenty-something white girl from Idaho strolls down Flatbush Extension peering into an open Mac Book in broad daylight, while a black man in Nation of Islam garb walks right past her. The 2011 remix of Brooklyn has people actually thinking that because those two people co-exist, they also commingle. If patrons of urban revitalization and proponents of this new, safe, and homogenized NYC ever bothered to "troop it" (ride the local subway to the last stop and take two buses), they'd end up in the far reaches of the city and the surrounding counties to get a dose of life outside of the bubble. It's when they complete their 90 minute commute, take off their DKNY shades, and peer over their shoulders that they'll encounter what everyone inside the bubble is thinking, but not doing. Depending on who they are and where they are, strange looks, blank stares, and a heightened sense of awareness will be all they find.

Despite Queens' status as a United Nations borough, brothers never could and still can't go to Howard Beach, you'll never get cursed out in Japanese in Rosedale, and you'll never find transient yuppies living in Cambria Heights until they decide to ditch the $65-a-day Whole Foods juice cleanses for jerk oxtail.

In many ways, this place is as segregated as the belly of the Deep South and it always has been. Many recent arrivals to the Big City of Dreams have difficulty believing me when I speak of high school cafeteria race riots in the '80s, the real estate agent-fueled polarizing of Long Island's bedroom suburbs, or the city of Yonkers' staunch refusal to desegregate its public schools and housing until being ordered by the court to do so in the late 1980s.

All I have to say to those who believe in all seriousness that NYC is a true melting pot is go out and try to play a social game of *Twister* in different areas of the city - see where it gets you. After six years of field study (and about 8,227 miles on my car), I can honestly say that it's pointless to mill around in any given NYC social "scene" for more than 15 minutes unless you call that scene home. Everyone is so face deep in their own convoluted reality, that an outsider is handled with tongs. The disconnect is parallel with Khalid Muhammad and Jennifer Aniston alone at a Woolworth's lunch counter discussing interracial dating over plates of bean pies and bacon. I will also say that it's a Haley's Comet occurrence that anything worthwhile happens after midnight except for the occasional drunk girl fight.

One particular weekend about four years ago will always be etched into my brain as Another Wasted Night. Every stereotype about every enclave I passed through rung about 97 percent true. Today, the same generalizations ring true. Then again, I'm not making generalizations, but…no, fuck that, I'm generalizing.

Stop #1: Home (Jamaica, Queens)

As a kid, I knew I would come back to my grandparents' home to live and build my studio. It's only right; this is the place where I first discovered music. Rochdale, Queens is a black, working-class section of South Jamaica, closer to Long Island than just about any other area of NYC in appearance and distance. Public transportation is limited to hourly Long Island Railroad service

140

and a few sketchy bus lines that never seem to come on time, if at all. It hasn't changed too much since white flight left that dust cloud on it in the early '70s; I doubt there will be a Whole Foods popping up anytime soon. I don't mind shoveling snow for the old folks on my block, but old folks are just about the only people worth talking to over here for any length of time. A good percentage of the few young adults left over here are only good for about 15 minutes of conversation before we veer into rap gossip (the new *Smack* DVD or the whereabouts of Bang 'Em Smurf), Superhead's latest dick-sucking adventure, or some shitty Tyler Perry movie that unfortunately left the cutting room floor.

"Yo Jay, you be on the creep man, where you been at?" asks Rasheem, a cat from my neighborhood. "I ain't seen your high-yellow ass in a minute."

I explain that I was in Europe doing gigs, and after an "aight aight" the subject changes immediately. Why? Because if you aren't on BET or World Star Hip-hop, nobody around here gives a fuck. If you can't brag about it in the barbershop, it has zero significance. Nobody over here is the least bit curious about me attempting to drive in Australia with the wheel on the opposite side of the car; it's just not on their radar. When you admit that you've eaten sushi or banged a girl with a flat ass in Europe, all you get is, "you on that other shit, you nasty son!" I realize that the conversation has peaked and I try to break north, but we're interrupted by a girl with a fat ass walking by.

"Yo shortay! Yo ma, lemme holla at you real quick!" Rasheem shouts. "Yo Jay, holla at that. You gay, nigga?"

I've never known a girl worth a bottle of Colt 45 backwash that would respond to "Yo Shorty!", so I don't say shit. Then, he informs me that the crew is rollin' down to the strip club tonight. He passes me a flyer with a picture of a Patra-looking chick with a delicious ass in mid-Bogle move. Looks good, but I decline.

"Yo son, you gotta be gay! You ain't hollerin' at these chicks out here, you ain't fuckin' with the strip club? Nigga, what the fuck do you do?!"

I then explain to Rasheem that I'm not gay, but I don't see the point in lap dances. Strip clubs are a financially stupid way of catching blue balls. If you need further explanation of why they're a bad move, ask Pac-Man Jones. I'll jerk off free of charge, and then throw my dollars at my Con Edison bill. I'll only throw dollars at one of those bitches if I can get them back at the end of the night.

"You my nigga Jay, but you're on that other shit!"

I give Rasheem a pound and try to see where I'll head next in my socially motivated game of *Twister*. I make a few phone calls and get some invites.

StOP #2: SOME LOFt PArty in WiLLiamSburg, BrOOKLYn

This is a 15-mile drive for me. The whole time I'm driving, I'm mumbling to myself, "This shit better be worth it." As I drive through "East Williamsburg" (formerly Bushwick, soon to be E.W.I.L.L. or some stupid-ass acronym that solely means the local bodega became a wi-fi café) I can't help but think to myself:

People pay $5,000 a month to live in these beat up ass ex-factories with 22 other people and the shower stall is in the middle of the living room? Smooth.

I arrive at the party and do my best to mingle. There's a metro-sexually-tinged thrift shop fashion sense in here and the DJ just threw on a God awful mash-up of a Lil' Wayne song and some '80s pop tune. I pause and reminisce about the one time I did a show over here and got semi-booed for coming out on stage to a Big Tymer$ song, but here we are a few years later. Sure enough, there are people walking around in extra medium Trap or Die t-shirts and wearing sunglasses indoors at midnight. I gotta drain the weasel, so I run to the bathroom and I really don't like what I see when I get there. Obviously all 300 of the people that live in this loft share one bathroom, so I guess it makes sense that the toilet bowl has a mysterious tan ring around it. I've been to quite a few of these loft parties; this tan ring around the bowl shit is a common theme. There's also some hair in the sink; this is totally my kind of party dude!

I step out into the party and make small talk with some broad with a flat and wide ass drinking a Pabst Blue Ribbon beer and sporting a t-shirt that has a defunct breakfast cereal on it. She tells me she's a vegan that only goes organic, and that goes for that American Spirit cigarette she's puffing on too. She asks where I live, so after explaining where Jamaica, Queens is (in relation to JFK Airport, the only Queens point of reference any current "New Yorker" seems to know besides the Beer Garden in Astoria) she responds with, "Daaamn, how do you live without the subway?!" I retort with, "Daaamn, how do you live with alternate side parking and late night track construction?!"

After I explain to her that there is indeed life beyond the Broadway Junction stop on the L train line, point out that Westchester County is not "upstate", and remind her that people do actually live on Staten Island, in Eastern Queens, and other communities that are remote from the subways (noting that her sanitation man is probably one of them), she tells me about her new dog and how much she loves to travel. She's making soporific small talk to acquiesce me, but her insouciance reeks in her facial expressions; she really couldn't give less of a fuck about anything I'm saying.

"Well, it's nice to meet you, I'm happy to be an official NYC girl now!" she says in closing. No bitch, you're a Vermont girl who bought "Empire State of Mind" on iTunes and crashes on someone's couch in Bed-Stuy. When you fall asleep on the A train and miss your stop, sweetie, be sure to text me when you wake up at the Mott Ave. station in Far Rockaway after dark. I want to be there to watch your "official" NYC street smarts and internal NYC GPS system kick in.

Then, a guy in a pair of $400 Flight Club retro sneakers walks by. I notice that he has a Crack Is Back shirt on. I ask him about Keith Haring's original *Crack Is Wack* anti-drug mural in Harlem that the shirt tried to put a negative spin on. He doesn't know what I'm referring to, because he just moved here from Utah and finished his graphic arts study at Pratt University. Ah, I get it now, he's going for irony. The emo-indie rock fan boy blogger becomes Young Jeezy all of a sudden, that's so fuckin' creative!

I've had a crackhead relative show up at a family function and it was a seminar in fear to say the least, so I ask him if he's also had the honor.

"Nah, but the shirt is fresh," he spat back.

I know "crack" is slang term that's widely used in entertainment, like "dope" is. But it's agonizingly obvious that listening to too many Clipse songs has caused this little guy to talk out of his ass. When the crack epidemic was ravaging neighborhoods like the one we were standing in at that moment, he was a mere toddler on the farm and his feet were too small to have any sneakers worth being stabbed for. After he calls Queens, Long Island, and Westchester "the 'burbs" (in a tone that suggested that maybe he was calling those places soft), I just laugh. I'm hoping that one day he makes a pit stop in Wyandanch, Mount Vernon, Hollis, or New Cassel and lets his guard down when he sees the *Leave It to Beaver*-style homes with the neatly kept lawns. Of course it won't be long before someone emerges from a dainty Tudor style house and pops a cap in his ass for looking out of place. For now though, I'll let the little fucker blindly enjoy the experience of living a mile from where Biggie Smalls sold crack and rolled dice without living in fear of being murdered for a Starter jacket.

A decent-looking chick walks by, but she's sloppy drunk and screaming the words to Kanye's "Stronger" in my face. I'd rather thrash the bitch than bone her at this point, so after a whopping 26 minutes, I'm ready to leave. Maybe if I had never quit drinking, I could stretch it to an hour.

143

StoP #3: SOME HOUSE PaRty in PaRK SLoPE, BroOKLyn

My ex-girl was invited to a party thrown by her little yuppie co-worker. I stop by to pick her up, but it would be rude of me to just come and go, right? My ex (who was Japanese) can't see that this party full of upward-nosed, newly-transplanted-to-Brooklyn snobs have made her the designated photographer, but won't offer her any drinks or talk to her beyond giving orders. I mention this and she gets mad. To end the arguing, I allow myself to get dragged into small talk with her co-worker and her Alex P. Keaton tool of a boyfriend. I don't expect the conversation to last long. Somehow, the purpose of doo-rags comes up. Of course this was after they deduce that I am indeed a black man, because I'm not "black like 50 Cent black, he's black."

I used to joke with friends about how being seen as the "non-threatening black guy" will cause conversation like this to fall out of the sky when "liberal" white folks who have never been around black folks decide that they no longer have to hide the silverware and get a little too cozy. The girl will ramble on about how she voted for Obama and divulge her dislike for Sarah Palin. The guy will claim he's a closet Lil' Jon fan. I have more respect for a man waving a Confederate flag than a makeshift "liberal" with a rap guilty pleasure who wouldn't come to Southeast Queens to visit me anyway. Sarah Palin would behave like an ignorant redneck to my face, but my chances of fuckin' her after a few beers would be exponentially greater than laying the pipe to soap box Becky who's telling me fur is wrong.

I went to school with folks like this, but in 1993 we both got in where we fit in. Now that Brooklyn is the hip spot, here they come - to a neighborhood that was merely another place to avoid after the sun went down. In 2011, they pass judgment on anybody who doesn't live there and participate in that cockamamie text message network for open parking spots. Over the course of 18 years, their open snobbishness has morphed into an NYC-customized faux-liberal outer layer – and it stinks.

"We live near where they filmed *The Cosby Show!*"

I know that already, you fuckin' cunt mouth. I answer their question about doo-rags. Then (like I did in the eighth grade when the blonde girl in my gym class started touching my Gumby haircut and asking me how I kept it in place) I ask them, "How do you make your hair straight like that without a hot comb?" They don't know how to react, and neither does my ex, who then leaves with me and chews me out in the car for being "inappropriate". As a native of Japan, I can't blame her for not understanding the snide, Pepto-Bismolcoated racism and class discrimination that stinks up the "hip" and nouveau enclaves of NYC today.

StOP #4: "GrOWn-N-SeXY" EVent, MidtOWn Manhattan

Mid-90's Bad Boy era hip-hop and R&B blasting inside, plenty of chicks with fat asses lined up outside - on paper it looks better than it is. I'm gauging the scene from the line but the dickhead bouncer, who is a dead giveaway for Kay Slay, starts beefing.

"No sneakers and no Tims, bruh. White on white Air Force Ones or shoes only."

Nigga please. For a $30 door cover, I should be allowed to wear whatever the fuck I want. A pair of white on white AF1s on my feet is a guarantee that I won't go in there and start grabbing asses and throwing bottles, you know. I have a pair of shoes in the car, so I go get them and come back to bite the bullet on the door charge like an idiot because fuck it, I feel there's nothing else to do. My friend's 30th birthday party is going on inside, so that's a dollar for each year. Of course 70 percent of the women in here are straight out of a Diddy video, but if you ain't buying drinks and looking hustler fresh, you'll be with your hand tonight.

Whenever I hear these docked yacht party-going Negroes claim they're getting their Grown-n-Sexy on today, I flash back to the flyer for this particular club, which sported the phrase Grown-n-Sexy in bold 18 point Impact font next to some made-for-BET movie-looking couple. So you cut your hair short, started shopping at Kohl's, look like Rick Fox, and now have an iPod full of quiet storm R&B instead of rap. Nigga please, you're still a fuckin' punk.

After being told my afro was "so cool" by a white chick at the loft party earlier, I'm told I need a haircut "badly" by a Nia Long-looking broad in here. I guess in the land of "Grown-n-Sexy", an atypical black hairstyle means you ain't "grown".

I chat briefly with some chick who looks pretty decent. It takes a mere two minutes for the broad to pop my favorite question.

"So what do you do for a living?" she finally spills.

At this point, the idea of going home, jerking off, and going to sleep was more appealing than any further social interaction of any type for the rest of the night. If I told the bitch that I worked at White Castle, would she say, "It was nice meeting you" and skedaddle, ask me why there are holes in White Castle burgers, or still take the time to get to know me as a person? For the most part, telling a woman at a Grown-n-Sexy party that I was a struggling musician throughout my 20s had the same effect as telling her I stole stock car stereos for a living.

After 30 minutes of evil return stares from chicks I make eye contact with that can tell I have no money and probably notice that I'm sporting Ralph Lauren Chaps instead of real Polo, I'm again ready to leave. "Gadget Hoes", "Flash Hoes", and "Huddle Hoes" are all out in full force; I've had enough. It's now 3AM and I've spent the last six hours fighting to find parking spots, fighting through Houston Street traffic, and fighting to stay interested in different scenes of NYC. I've also dinged up my axle just a tad more on Atlantic Ave. on the way home and put 57.2 useless miles on my ride, which is the place I spent most of my time in just getting to the functions. I even pass by the local strip club Rasheem told me about earlier. A brawl had broken out and it got shut down early. Hey, at least the dude who got cracked in the dome with a Hennessy bottle won't be falsely accused of being gay.

Ignore thy neighbor

Why can't we all just get along and be one big picnic-in-Prospect Park-having, hand-holding city? Because the world's greatest city is filled to capacity with residents who are only aware of what's on the tip of their noses.

For a city that prides itself on diversity and variety, the greater NYC area is the most deceptively segregated area in America. I've actually come to utilize these fruitless nights for laughter purposes. Although every part of this city has some alright people, every "scene" itself is pathetic. I've gotten a few cheap and trampy one night stands out of this field study, but I wish I had stayed home 90 percent of the time. This is why nowadays you can find me hanging with the elderly folks in my neighborhood. Hearing their secrets to a successful marriage are pimpishly hilarious ("young brother, you gots to lay that pipe to the broad, no matter how bad the arthritis is kickin' in!") and their opinions hold more weight than someone who has never been north of 42nd Street, east of Broadway Junction, or south of Prospect Park telling me that racism doesn't exist here because we're a blue state. They also hold more weight than someone who never left Southeast Queens speaking of strip clubs like they were just invented or some Sarah Jessica Parker knock-off bitch claiming "Bed-Stuy Brooklyn!" with volume, but she never attended a basketball game at Boys & Girls High School.

Four years after my wasted night, NYC has continued to move along the path it was trudging at the time. Urban renewal of areas that are commuter friendly with Manhattan has spread deeper into Brooklyn, Queens, and even over the Hudson River.

How about in Jersey City, NJ last year, where a party I was invited to was broken up by neighbors calling the police to squash the noise?

"C'mon dude, the music isn't bothering anyone," some guy wearing his little sister's pants told the cop. "Lighten up."

But at 1AM on a slowly-changing block that was still predominantly working class, the longtime resident neighbors were the ones who called the fuzz. They were trying to get some fuckin' sleep so they could rise early and open up their stores for this clown to stumble into later on that day to buy a bottle of smart water. No, you lighten up, asshole.

It was also evident on a cold March morning in 2008, as I watched a pack of young women holding Saks Fifth Avenue shopping bags, giggling loudly, and wearing DKNY coats frolic through Bed-Stuy like it was their college campus.

"Go back where you came from white bitches!" screamed a junior high age kid on a dirt bike, as he rolled by clad in a hoodie and a baseball hat too big for his head.

The knucklehead Brooklyn teenager versus the transient stranger is a tension that's a by-product of NYC's revitalization efforts. These people share a neighborhood in the midst of transformation, but neither cares nor understands how the other lives. The same can be said of Rasheem and the flat and wide-assed girl at the loft party. He only knows and respects what's in tennis ball-throwing distance of his front stoop and she would never care enough to ask her postman, cab driver, or sanitation man what's going on in their respective neighborhoods.

Meanwhile, people in Park Slope bitch about a commute to Williamsburg to see their lover because there's no common train line to connect the two gentrified neighborhoods that are a mere three miles apart. Life sucks because they have to journey into Manhattan and back into Brooklyn to sit around and discuss their old lives in Wisconsin. Folks in the brand new, picturesque, Arverne by the Sea developments in Far Rockaway, Queens love their scenic view of the Atlantic Ocean. When they have to catch the A train or get some yogurt from the local Stop & Shop though, they're face to face with longtime residents from the other side of the tracks who've been posted up in the public housing of former NYC Mayor John Lindsay's forgotten dumping ground for the last 40 years. Hasidic Jews thwart hipsters' attempts to re-paint bike lanes in their overlapping neighborhoods. Longtime friends move to different boroughs, and suddenly their entire relationship is based on Facebook comments. Jane from Kansas calls Harlem "Northern Manhattan" now, and it's pretty ironic. That "Harlem World, Uptown represent, stop bein' playa hater, Cristal bottles are poppin' and we ain't stoppin'" banter from rappers of the mid-'90s was pretty God damn flossy, but the braggarts couldn't stop Jane and her buddies from taking over the block.

NYC is one big, subdivided, surface level, oblivious, and ignorantly happy city. In its current state, it's no longer that much greater than any other major city in America. Melting pot my ass, but I'll be damned if we don't have the best restaurants.

HERE ARE SEVEN NYC SIGNS.
IF YOU CAN'T NAME THE BOROUGHS
THEY'RE IN, YOUR NYC IQ IS LOW...

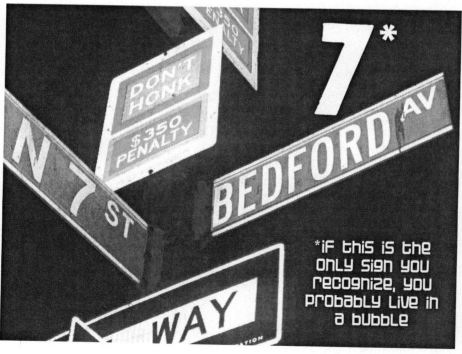

*if this is the only sign you recognize, you probably live in a bubble

21. OUT FOR THE COUNT

"Bigamy is having one husband or wife too many. Monogamy is the same." - Oscar Wilde

If you've tried to figure out the opposite sex, you've already lost. Men are dumb dogs; women are bat shit crazy; that's all we need to know. Trying to probe any further is comparable to a crackhead trying to operate a Boeing 747. The sooner we all realize that, the sooner we can see love as a gender driven boxing match and make the most of it. Round One:

The man and woman trade numbers, but neither wants to be the first to call. Some dummy implemented a "three day rule" before making a phone call many years ago, just so nobody seems desperate. Nowadays, you can add texting to the equation just to make things more flaky and indirect. Games. That's nothing but bobbing and weaving for style points and chasing each other around the ring, expending energy. The first punch landed is a date, and the fight intensifies. She wants to go see *Cats* on Broadway at the tune of $200 a ticket and he wants to stay home and watch the Knick game for free. He goes. That's called taking a jab on the nose. The male may be ahead of the game on the scorecard, so he bides time by doing more unnecessary bobbing and weaving, like trying to get on good terms with her friends that really don't like him anyway and think she deserves better. If the sex is good, someone has just been knocked down and forced to get back up to a ten count. This is getting dangerous.

"I love you," the woman says to the man for the first time. That's an uppercut to the ribs; chances are he wasn't expecting it and now he's out of air. When a man is caught off guard with that statement (we usually are) and he feels the woman actually means it, he can't react in the manner that she wants him to. He's in shock and was happy with where things were going, which was nowhere in particular. The man is stuck between being Joe Isuzu (selling the woman a lemon and telling her it's a new Maybach) and just being honest. He's fucked whichever way he goes, so he comes out with a happy medium response.

"Um. Thank you! You're a great person!"

That's a left hook to the chin - utterly undesirable and not what the woman wanted. It's completely unromantic, cryptic, and disgustingly safe for the seventh round of a fifteen round fight. The trend of peaks and valleys continues, with the goal being a draw after the fight goes the distance (a happy marriage and kids). However, more often than not, someone gets knocked the fuck out and the fight is over. Or, maybe the fight gets nasty and the referee then has to step in and end it, declaring a winner (better known as divorce court). Time to call Judge Mills Lane. 90 percent of the time, that's how dating goes in America. Shut the fuck up and accept it or bow out.

Dating "Rules"

There's nothing worse than going online and seeing articles like "What Turns Men Off on the First Date" or "What Women Really Want." Yawn. I browse through *Men's Health* magazine in the supermarket and every issue has a "Make Her Find You Irresistible" article advertised on the cover. Sigh. That shit doesn't apply to your monkey ass unless you're on the set of Universal Studios filming the latest delusional romantic comedy. Men want women to stay in shape and stop nagging. Women want men to be knights in shining armor and exhibit the perfect balance of excitement, manliness, intelligence, humor, sensitivity, and stability - with trace amounts of asshole tendencies sprinkled about for an element of danger. Right, and I want 8-track tapes to be the default music playing medium for the general public again, but how much luck do you think I'll have putting that one in effect?

Well, Can We Be Friends?

Friends? Bitch, do I look like Teddy Ruxpin to you? I've never known a man to desire a 100 percent platonic friendship with a good looking woman upon first meeting her. The platonic Friend Zone is equivalent to a day at the Department of Motor Vehicles with no air conditioning and a bunch of snot-nosed kids running around.

I don't think I can have sex with you, because I value our friendship too much.

Dropping that bomb on someone who's into you is the equivalent of the cops telling you your family dog of 27 years was just flattened by an 18-wheeler. Unless you've been friends with the person for so many eons

154

that you've embraced the friendship and are cool with that G-rated plateau, just spare your admirer the misery of a platonic friendship and skedaddle. Or, remain celibate, make every one of your admirers suffer equally, and inform them all that they're not alone.

WE LOVE TO LOSE

Will all men do a woman wrong? No. Are all men dogs? Yes. We all know a woman who complains about our canine ways, but she always goes back to her knucklehead ex-boyfriend, the biggest dog in the kennel. The whole thing is comparable to buying cars. A lot of women do the same thing – get with the male who represents the Honda Accord with lowest mileage at the best price. That's the stable, status quo car purchase for the average American. That candy apple red '64 Impala is what really tickles her fancy, but society told her the Honda was the best long term move. She'll dump the Honda for the Impala anyway, and when the Impala's transmission goes, she'll be back on the bus saying, "All cars ain't shit."

Women wonder why successful and intelligent men love sluts, jumpoffs, hookers, and home-wreckers. The answer is the same - the thrill of the chase and the presence of a challenge. We as men appreciate the Honda's reliability, but God damnit, we want to ride the Impala every now and then. We buy one car for daily needs, joy ride the other, crash 'em both, and wind up on the bus too.

Instead of using the most underutilized words in the English language when it comes to human interaction (no, never, and goodbye), we as humans love to prolong the unnecessary and dive head first into bullshit just to have more shit about the opposite sex to complain about. Both men and women love to lose.

Once that honeymoon phase ends, you're fucked. That's why I always liked Al Bundy on *Married with Children*. He and that redhead broad he was married to represent what 90 percent of marriages are like when the excitement is gone. The man becomes a lazy turd and finds solace in his frosty mug beer, recliner, and football game. The woman watches *Eat, Pray, Love* and decides that she's going to blow her life savings on $50,000 pilgrimages to India, Bali, and Italy to find herself. Barf. C'mon bitch, you're white, skinny, gainfully employed, and in good health. Bimbo, I worked in a high school where there was nothing to eat but frozen vegetables and ketchup, kids prayed they could stay out of shelters, and the only love was gang love.

LOVE t.K.O.

Famously Fucked: Why do Pro-athletes and Entertainers get Married?

I wish I knew the answer to this. These clowns have women in every city and they can afford to pay. When I say pay, keep in mind that no man really pays for the act of sex. Unless he's 80 years old or completely useless, he's usually paying to be left alone afterward.

Nate the Wino from around the corner cheated on his woman once, but he never got a God damn televised press conference to apologize. Now I have to turn on the tube and watch some simp that can swing a nine iron sit up there and apologize to the entire universe via press conference for leaving a sloppy ho trail. Fuck the fans and fuck the media, he gets paid to hit golf balls around, not to kowtow and explain himself to people who have no business caring about another man's dick history.

At one point, I believe Kelis was seeking 40 something grand a month in child and spousal support (plus legal fees) from Nas so she could maintain the lifestyle she was "accustomed" to during their marriage. Shit, that's the biggest God damn unemployment check I've ever seen. That's a "Thief's Theme" for your ass. And I'm up here mad because one of the dryers in the Laundromat ate my quarter last week. I'm sure Nas was "accustomed" to gettin' some head, but I wonder if a judge would ever make the continuance of fellatio a stipulation.

So Here We Are

When I say "we", I'm referring to anyone born before 1982 that is still single. Our happily (and unhappily) married and committed friends make attempts to hook us up with every other single person they feel sorry for. To make matters worse, they do it with the subtlety of a crossbow to the neck.

"It's about that time Jay," they'll warn me like a Tarot Card reader.

It's about that time for what? Hammertime? *Time* Magazine?

"Time to settle down, get a wife, some kids. You don't want to be the 40 year old man in the club." Shut up.

A disturbing number of Americans speak of their impending marriage and kids like they speak of a trip to their accountant to give Uncle Sam every last dime - like it's a necessary evil. Fuck it, go ahead and mail it in Mr. & Mrs. Postman.

I don't want to seem like I'm defective,

fuck it, I'm getting up in age. It's time.

It's safe to say that the biological clocks of man and womankind are the biggest culprits in failed marriages. That time clock cop out shit only works if you're 12 sizes bigger in the pants than you were in high school.

I'm not saying that it can't work, but almost everyone I've seen get married just said "fuck it," especially the men. That has to be the reason why healthy marriages are beginning to look like those early '90s haircuts with the dreadlocks that were skin faded on the side - you can only see them in video clips from the past.

Sometimes I wonder if my grandparents' 50 year monogamous marriage was an anomaly or merely a sign of the times. Divorce wasn't a pertinent option for irreconcilable differences in 1969. You either worked through your differences or accepted that your spouse had a side lover. These points and unanswered questions coupled with all the other nonsense I've seen and been through has led me to one solution - it may be time to take a trip to the sex shop and just call it a day.

- No more love related deaths.

- No more baby mama/baby daddy drama and waiting for test results.

- No more "If I can't have you, nobody can" crap.

- No more passive-aggressive behavior (i.e., "You don't care about me at all, but it's OK, haha, don't worry about it, I'll just suffer for you. I like doing that.")

- No more being a victim of reality TV, aka the deathblow to dating in America.

- No more dating site notification emails about some no tooth sloth broad named Ethel or some *Jerry Springer* candidate man with eight kids, and how she/he is your perfect match.

- No more hiding in the closet because your partner left out that little detail about living with their spouse and now you've been busted with your pants down.

- No more jealous exes or wild rumors involving your partner and the back of a UPS truck in 1998.

- No more being looked at like there *must* be something wrong with you because you're over 30 and still single.

Digital Underground had it right with the concept of Sex Packets in 1990. We won't even interact anymore after the year 2020, thanks to all of this faceless, technology-driven socializing. Pride is out, economizing is in.

Question: "Well what about companionship?"
Answer: "Get the fuck outta here."

Every woman is out walking a dog these days. I saw a broad kiss her dog on the God damn mouth, for fuck's sake. Men have been phased out already. They're sick of our bullshit, fellas; we've been replaced by Yorkies, we suck. Additionally, with communication in modern relationships being comprised of 90 percent texting, what type of companionship are you getting? That shit is a cop out; most couples haven't had any real companionship in ages. That's why I just ordered the first season of *227* on DVD, so I can watch Jackee and her titties jumping up and down for six hours; that's all the companionship I need today.

I can hear my boys talking to me now when I step into a club:

"Yo there's mad fine chicks in here Jay, holla at one."

Fuck that. Mr. Don't Holla is my name and staying drama-free is my game. I'm considering going on ho-atus and copping a blow-up doll. Whether I cave in and fall back into the world of relationships to try my luck or fully and permanently embrace my sexual alternative to Twitter remains to be seen. If you don't hear from me for a few years, it means that I'm at a gas station on an island somewhere inflating my new broad with an air hose. An air body beats an airhead any day.

In summation, spouses are like cars just as much as relationships are: You love them on first sight; they need constant maintenance to run smooth; your neighbor's always looks better; one wrong turn can wreck the whole shit; they don't make them like they used to; some folks go foreign for less headache; fly rims and a bad engine = a dope body on a psycho; a good tune up = make up sex; paying a fee to rent one for a night allows you to inflict the wear and tear that you couldn't inflict on your own; and it's better to dead them before they die so you can cut your losses.

22. A BROAD ABROAD

"my new used car is foreign, has low mileage, doesn't make a whole lot of noise, and plays cassettes. sounds like a craigslist ad for my future wife." - J-zone

The moment I saw it, it completely fucked me up and I'd never view dating in America the same way again.

As my Sleazy Listening tour partners and I were eating gyros and falafels in Gotenburg, Sweden, the greasy apron-wearing man slaving behind the deep-fryer closed down the little food hut and passed the key over to the manager. Out of the shadows emerged a woman so fine, you'd be subject to let her live if she walked into your house, took a squat, and pissed on your living room sofa for no reason. She gave our chef a Swedish French kiss, before the two danced off into the distance arm in arm.

"That's what I'm saying, that's some bullshit," I said to nobody in particular.

"What?" Vakill responded 10 seconds later, but I never explained to him what I meant.

I began to spot that scenario day in and day out as we trotted across Europe. People who didn't appear to make the most money, have the best job, or possess the highest level of education weren't phased out of the dating pool. I also noticed that in Australia when I went back in 2007. The more I saw it, the more adamant I became about purposely missing my flight home one day.

I came home from the Sleazy Listening tour to see a girl I was dating, who found it strange that I lived with and took care of my elderly grandmother.

"That must suck," she said in an arrogant deadpan. It was even more disturbing to be clicking with women, but they suddenly lost interest upon my telling them that I lived with my grandmother and my occupation was "rap musician." Thanks to Tyra Banks' jumbo forehead, reality TV, that mirage of the American Dream that Americans think really exists, and the four tramps on *Sex and the City*, dating in this country (and particularly in New York City) has become a waltz in a minefield. I've met a handful of incredible American women who had the capacity to think for themselves, but the majority of them needed dating Cliff's Notes written by a miserable somebody looking for company.

Online dating is an even bigger quagmire in this city. I laugh when I see broads with stratospheric expectations on dating websites letting it be known that they can't date a guy with a certain e-mail provider, a guy who shops at TJ Maxx, a guy who doesn't have at least a Ph.D., a guy who makes less than $50,000 a year, a guy whose passport doesn't have at least 15 stamps, a guy who lives more than two miles away, or a guy who doesn't have eight-pack abs. Most of them love to travel, need a man who can afford to jet set to Spain with them, and have *Eat, Pray, Love* listed in their favorite movies and books list. Okay sweetie, then you have to remain a size two with a Coke bottle shape and wrinkle-free skin after age forty. I will monitor every God damn French fry you put on your plate and call up the gym to see if you swiped in today. How you like them apples?

Instead of letting nature take its course, Americans try to map shit out like the kid who always played quarterback in a pick-up football game did when you were in grade school. He'd usually demonstrate what you were supposed to do on his hand or with a stick in the dirt.

Ronnie, you run to the middle of the field and cut right. Kirk, you run up the middle. Fat boy, you stay here and block. Richie and Hassan, y'all run deep to the end zone. If nobody is open, I'm running down the sideline, block for me. On hut four. Ready? Break!!

Americans, in my experience, do the same shit when it comes to relationships. You want X, Y, and Z in a relationship, huh? So, e-harmony divulged all of the secrets to a successful relationship last week and they make sense to you, huh? All of this info on a first date, huh? Whatever, you'd find a way to fuck a toaster oven if it made you feel like a million dollars, so quit using relationship self-help books as a Scantron for love advice. As stated earlier in this book, the most potent way to sell an idea or a service is via fear. We all fear loneliness, and that fear has turned dating into big business. It's all for naught though; giving relationship advice to Americans is like giving a man on his deathbed sousaphone lessons - just something to pass time before the inevitable.

.   Back in my own community, I'm even more assed out. Thanks to *Jet* magazine and those made-for-BET Shemar Moore movies, the image of the successful black man is usually a corporate brother who listens to current R&B and looks like he belongs on the front of a razor bump cream container, but it's eventually discovered that he's a "playa" anyway. Regardless, he'll have better chances than I will. I may be a decent cat beneath it all, but I'm also blue collar, quirky, and walking around with a very "un-grown man-like" haircut. I watch old episodes of *McCloud* in my spare time and listen to Tim Dog in my car; those are enough deal breakers to completely disqualify me from dating 90 percent of the women in the Black American dating pool. The only concept more unfathomable in the black community than self-deprecation is eccentricity. Let me show up to the block walking arm in arm with an Asian or white chick, though; the teeth-sucking ensemble will start immediately. Yes, the good ol' sucking of teeth. The alphabet actually has 27 letters for most of the women in my neighborhood; the teeth-suck sound is now officially the letter between 's' and 't'. Keep up the good work, hoodrats.

It's almost a bad thing to be exposed to the level playing field that a good chunk of the world operates on though, because it makes your return to the United States that much more of a root canal.

An hour after my disturbing realization at the Swedish gyro hut, I met Nadine, who completely threw me for a loop. She was pretty, but what impressed the most about her was the fact that she learned to speak perfect English by buying and listening to rap music over the years. One of the albums that was part of her self-applied ESL curriculum was none other than Tim Dog's *Penicillin on Wax*, my favorite rap album of all time. Getting a piece of information like that is enough to make a man like me throw his bachelor card in the shredder. The likelihood of finding an American woman who can appreciate the song "Fuck Compton" is about the same as finding a Polish woman who can burn the shit out of some collard greens and candied yams.

It was refreshing to hear a completely uninhibited Nadine call men "bitches and hoes," talk about how some guy she knew was "a pussy with no dick," and go completely Dice Clay on me five minutes after meeting her. On the opposite side of the token, it was also pretty damn cool to hear views on racism and politics in America from an outsider who gave a shit. I've never been the type to walk on eggshells around women, but I felt an alarming level of comfort and freedom to pop off at the mouth around Nadine. I've never met anyone cut from that same cloth at home.

A few months prior to the Sleazy Listening tour, I met a spunky little tomboy chick in Amsterdam when I did the Fat Beats ten-year anniversary show. Homegirl was clad in fatigues, combat boots, and a tank top; I can admit

163

I was a little intimidated by her at first. We went out and had the kind of night that would end up in a cheap '80s flick about sex, drugs, and rock and roll. She made sure I got as high as the gas prices of summer 2008 on a 30 Euro budget, and when her work was done, she sent me home with scratches, hickeys, bloodshot eyes, back spasms, and a grin on my face that even the customs agent had to laugh at.

"I don't need to see your passport," he said with an accompanying smirk. "That's an Amsterdam face."

The good ol' internet allowed my Amsterdam vixen and I to reconnect in America years later. When we hung out, she brought the red carpet with her. We hit the Caesars Palace Mall in Las Vegas, where she was originally from. While strolling around the mall, she asked me to buy her some lingerie and a $200 dinner; I went down to the slot machines, jerked off, and went to sleep instead. The girl's modus operandi did a 180 degree flip based on her settings. In Amsterdam, you make the most of what you've got; in Vegas, you get what you pay for.

The fact that you can be "out of your league" in so many instances over here means that there's a problem to begin with. Ultimately, when women get sick of going to clubs, can't shed those love handles, and no longer find fun in rejecting people on dating sites because of their taste in movies, they finally begin to behave. When men reluctantly succumb to the "I don't want to be the old man in the club" fear, they follow suit in a half-assed manner. I could just kick back, grab a Bartles & Jaymes premium wine cooler, and wait for the magical day when everyone falls into place with 30 extra pounds to sport, but I'll just stick with my hand and two minutes of my time instead.

Women abroad were also more desirable because they didn't stigmatize sex like it was some taboo act that only Prince Charming was entitled to. Chicks from London were particularly brassy in my experience. They made no bones about saying, "I want you to fuck the living shit out of me." They wouldn't call the police if you told them, "I want to fuck the shit out of you" first, either. Only in America do men and women need a reason to fuck beyond the fact that they both want to fuck. All that wining and dining is a bunch of smoke and mirrors for what two animals were put here to do anyway.

So now the new NYC chick you met is working on her Ph.D., hits snob wine and cheese parties in her spare time, and has too much couth to stomach a dirty joke. She stuck you in the Friend Zone because you're not on pace to be in her tax bracket or level of paper education, but she failed to let you know that your chances are nonexistent. One day, she'd like to get married and live the American Dream, but that's only with the man behind Door #2, not you.

164

What the hell does all of that balderdash have to do with you and her fuckin'? Zilch. She wants to fuck too, but our American bubble has trained us to play these games under the guises of self-respect and control. There's nothing more unnerving than a room full of stiffs who really want to fuck, but they're too busy downing Cosmos, playing games, and texting people who aren't around so they can appear disinterested and interesting at the same time.

As I sat in the car last year and watched my man Mike's hoodrat girl-friend barbecue him about not buying her an outfit for the club, I analyzed the nature of his situation. Was he unfortunate for eating Happy Meals throughout his entire life and not knowing that T-Bone steaks are available in other places around the world? Maybe I was the unlucky duckling. I tasted the T-bone steak, only to have it snatched away and have a Happy Meal waiting for me when I taxied down the runway at JFK Airport.

23. ARE MEN THE NEW WOMEN (WHAT THE FUCK)?

"What are you, bitch, a boy or a girl?" - Willie D

One day back in 1998, I was thumbing through my record collection and buggin' off the outfits worn by the bands on their album covers. My childhood aspirations of playing in a funk band meant that I had a fair share of late '70s albums with covers that featured the most androgynous fashion mankind has ever seen. These covers were eyesores, some displaying what an auto collision involving Prince and a Mister Softee truck might look like. I took a peek into the small crate of hair metal I had acquired while looking for stadium rock drum samples. If the funk and disco album jackets were nauseating, the hair metal covers were just plain noxious. Thankfully this was all a decade-plus into the past.

"That's one look that ain't never coming back," I assured myself. Oops.

Eleven years later (as I squeezed past a very dainty-looking man holding an umbrella on Broadway on a day where not a single cloud sat in the sky) I was trying to fathom the mindset behind Fashion Week in New York City. Yes, we (along with Paris, London, and Milan) always fiend to show extra special love to genderless dress codes. Understanding the allure of it all is like completing a crossword puzzle with no vowels in it.

If you're on stage or in a fashion show, fine, anything goes in those settings. But on the streets of big cities like New York, people are trying to outdo each other with the most perplexing fashion statements they can think of. I'm all for setting new tradition, but walking through Soho feels like walking smack dead into Boy George's video shoot.

After my PC was thrashed with malware for the umpteenth time, I ventured down to the Apple Store to price Macs. Men with taco meat on the chest and fur on the feet walking around in skin tight V-Neck sweaters with no undershirt and open toe sandals looking like Teen Wolf went metro seemed to be the norm. I'm scared to go back to Soho to buy that Mac; I think I'd rather buy another PC at Best Buy and withstand the virus hassles than be exposed to that fashion quagmire again.

Even the kids are sliding down the dark tunnel of androgyny. For the record, I have nothing against fads; today's kids have their own shit just like we had ours. In high school in the early '90s, my generation wore our pants way off our asses and eight sizes too big like we were fresh out of Spofford, so adults said the same shit about us. In retrospect, we looked incredibly stupid, but at least we could let our nuts hang to the left (or right) so they could breathe a little bit. However, if you were to ask some kid posting up in his lo-rise spandex denim, "How's it hangin' man?" in 2011, he'd respond, "It's stuck dude."

There's nothing wrong with being well-groomed and fashionable, but I really want to figure out what drives a man's desire to out-pretty a woman if he's not an actual pimp. Only the silkiest of pimps are in competition to be pretty, so unless your name is Suga Free, Goldie, or Pretty Tony, I don't see the motivation. I've also seen quite a few men carrying designer granny purses lately. Excuse me, "murses," aka male purses. Was Indiana Jones ahead of his time? I understand that with the influx of all these new pointless gadgets, you may need something to carry all your shit around and don't want to roll with a briefcase out of fear of looking like your pops or haul a backpack out of fear of looking like you're about to start freestyling. Nonetheless, there are other viable options besides a big purse with a giant pink unicorn outlined in diamond studs on it.

People in the fashion world accuse me of intolerance, ignorance, or whatever "ance" you feel would apply to old-school thinking. Many just call me a hater. I was raised in the 1980s and early '90s, when haters didn't exist. Back then, it was called having an opinion. In my opinion, this whole "let's rehash the glam rock dress code and drag it a step further into the cavern of androgyny" thing stinks.

I remember opening the August 2nd, 2009 Sunday Edition of the NY Daily News and spotting a center spread of men showing off dainty designer bags with $3,000 price tags that you would expect Naomi Campbell to have slung over her shoulder. All of a sudden, the plight of Plaxico Burress facing prison time in the sports section didn't seem too serious to me. No, I'm not being insecure, I'm just puzzled. Some things are made for men and some things are made for women, like purses.

Here's my first question: What the fuck is in that big purse that a man would need on his way to Starbucks from the office? A wallet, keys, a cell phone, some chewing gum, and maybe some glasses. What else can you stuff in something that big and stylish? Multiple choices:

a. a Teddy Ruxpin doll
b. Radio Raheem's cassette single of "Fight the Power"
c. Arvid from *Head of the Class'* pocket protector
d. The tissue Redman used to stuff in his nose when his first album came out
e. Theo Huxtable's homemade Gordon Gartrelle shirt

Maybe the ever thinning line between genders has something to do with men and women not understanding each other and men seeking to relate. Maybe some of these dainty-ass men just want to go undercover to get some info and bring it back to the home base. If that's the case, some of these men look so convincingly feminine they could give Sonny Spoon a run for his cash in the disguise department.

Here is my next question: Is there an unfair double standard against tomboys? All of these *Vogue*-reading fashion "experts" will tell a woman in baggy sweats and Timberland boots to "grow up and dress like a lady" with no hesitation. But if you tell this frail-by-nature and still counting his carbohydrates so he can out-slim his girlfriend waif of a "man" in ankle warmers - ankle warmers are my term for skinny jeans that you can't pull past your thigh - to "grow your little milquetoast bitch ass up dress like a God damn man," then you're intolerant, archaic, ignorant, immature, and insecure. I'm wondering how long it will be before I'm no longer relevant in the social landscape because I can't brag to the fellas about the clearinghouse price I bought my new bra for.

As I explained earlier in this book, men and women aren't supposed to share all of the same traits, nor should we attempt to relate to each other. If we did, we'd all be one gender, for fuck's sake. Once again, men and women are chitterlings and tofu, Ernie and Bert, Felix and Oscar, etc. If you can wear your girlfriend's clothes beyond you sleeping in that way too big t-shirt she has in the bottom of her drawer that she uses for a nightgown, that's a terrible thing. Let me see if I can figure out an answer to all of this shit; I'll bet $5,600.

(Insert Jeopardy theme music here)

The fuck if I know, I just lost $5,600. I give up and that's my final answer.

PArt thrEe: woRd to The nErd

real macks play 8-tracks

24. ADVENTURES IN DIGGIN'

"I dig like coal miners through the crates of old timers." - Tash of Tha Alkaholiks

Your girlfriend will never understand you dragging her into an asthma-inducing dump of a store to sit patiently while you sift through some damn records. Meanwhile, she falls into a coughing fit. Virgin lungs. When a man is into digging for records, he puts his health (and life) on the line every day, building a tolerance. I haven't known anybody to die in the line of duty, but some of us have knocked a few years off our lives by inhaling mold and funny looking dusts that can't possibly be OSHA approved. Some people fly to strange countries solely to dig, but I never went that far; I have bills to pay. Believe it or not, I've gone record hunting on three different continents and my best stories are from local spots and junk yards right here in America. Sometimes it's all about the experience, not the records.

My addiction to scouring through record bins started in about the fourth grade (1987), a good year or two before I was even buying rap music. After discovering my folks' old funk albums as a kid, I became a completist of a hand full of '70s funk bands. At the time, most of these records were 10 to 20 years old, but there was no internet and no high profile dealers, so joints that reside in the dollar bins (or have since made their way to iTunes) today were much harder to find then. I was spending all of my $10 a week allowance on records, so every ring I scrubbed from around the bathtub in my mom's apartment was another dollar to throw at a record with a wild, afro-dotted album cover. I also started playing bass guitar around this time, so of course funk records gave me the best shit to emulate.

As time went on, my habit got more expensive. By the time I was in my Vee-Dubbs studio days, I was in a higher salary bracket. I had also begun to make beats, and the need for samples jacked my habit up to a $100 a week fix. When you're 17 years old with no responsibility, you can afford that.

With 24 years of crate digging experience under my belt, here are ten record spots that stood out amongst the rest:

10. Greenline Records - Queens, NY (Defunct)

This was the first record store I ever called home; I nearly paid rent there from 1987 to 1989. It was on Guy R. Brewer Blvd. in South Jamaica, Queens, about three miles from my house. Greenline had been around for ages; my pops used to go there to buy jazz when he was in high school. So when I was trying to find Bohannon's *Stop & Go* album (which is still a hard find to this day) and complete my collection for the group Slave but couldn't pin down two of their releases, my pops suggested Greenline. When you walked into the joint, it was raggedy. It had an arcade game in the front and a few glass display cases, some with cassettes and one with 8-track tapes for the local pimps who never updated their Cadillacs. There was an older man with glasses and another dude with a curly fro and a denim jacket who was a dead ringer for Lee Oskar from War. They took me to a Slave section that was about one foot thick. Three and four coffee-stained copies of every album they ever released were right in front of my face. He pulled the last copy of the *Stop & Go* record out of an even bigger Bohannon stack, while looking at me funny, like 'what the hell is this little kid doing buying records that are older than he is?'

For the next two years, every penny of my allowance was spent in Greenline. As I got older, I found other stores and got into record conventions, but Greenline remains king. Every time I pass where it was, I stop and nod. Being that Studio 1212 was around the corner, Ultramagnetic, the late Paul C, and a teenage Large Professor all did work in that spot. The last time I was in there was 1999, when I was working on my *A Bottle of Whup Ass* EP. I copped a few jazz records that I wound up sampling and Dick Hyman's *Moon Gas* LP for $10. Greenline closed a year later.

9. Records Unlimited - New Rochelle, NY (Defunct)

Records Unlimited was on a tougher section of the main drag (North Avenue) in New Rochelle. I would get my hi-top fade cut at Al's Barber Shop, which was around the corner from this spot. It didn't look all that dingy, so I never went in there much. But when I started to collect hip-hop and hip-house records around '89, I started going in there to get 12" singles. That's when I discovered the nice selection of funk they had. Along with my cameo haircut, I was also collecting the funk band Cameo's early shit around this time; Records Unlimited had an insane selection of early Cameo. I bagged Kool & the Gang's *Light of Worlds* LP in there for $6 after seeing it a month prior at rip-off-ass Colony Records in Manhattan for $30. The last record I bought in there was The Ohio

Players' *Pleasure* album. A month later, I passed by it on the Bee-Line #61 bus and it was boarded up. The next time I slid to that area to get a haircut, I walked over and asked some dread standing in front of the neighboring Goffman's bodega (an ultra-hood and defunct New Ro hangout) what happened to Records Unlimited. He just shook his head.

"The IRS," he mumbled. "They didn't pay their bills, mon." Bloodclot!

8. Breakdown Records - Queens, NY

I needed to get my mother a birthday gift and I didn't know what the hell to buy. There was a shitload of traffic on the Cross Island Parkway, so my father and I took the local streets through Queens and passed this shop in the Bayside area. All record stores were worth being investigated around that time, so I took the plunge and was pleasantly surprised when I trotted through the door. Not only did I pick up a Marvin Gaye LP for $3 for mom dukes, but I found Kool & the Gang's *Music Is the Message* LP for $4. With my mother playing "Jungle Boogie" around the apartment during my early childhood, I was always a Kool fan (primarily their mid-70's stuff), but I didn't know about their rarest (and best) material from 1969-72. On the back cover, the band printed pictures of their previous four albums. When I saw that they existed, the chase was on (it would take a year before I found them all in 1990).

I found a cover-less original copy of the elusive *Mulatu of Ethiopia* record there in the late '90s. It was in a junk crate by the door getting ready to be picked up by sanitation. Breakdown is also stuffed to the gills with obscure VHS and cassette tapes. I scored KMD's *Mr. Hood*, Son of Bazerk's album, and a handful of Rap-A-Lot Records releases all sealed in their original cardboard CD long boxes.

Twenty years later, Breakdown is still standing. The owner, Anthony, is a cool cat; every record in the store is $2. Breakdown was cluttered throughout my hardest digging days, but these days it's well-kept and fairly organized. Chances are slim that tourists and current NYC transients will ever see it, though. One would have to hop the LIRR, drive, or take a handful of buses to get there. As soon as you're talking two and three fare zones to Nouveau Yorkers, they lose their sense of adventure all of a sudden. Mo' for me.

7. New York City Record Convention – Manhattan (Defunct)

This wasn't a spot, but an event that was held either at the Roosevelt Hotel or in Union Square a few times a year. By 1993, selling beats was big business and dealers were digging up samples to sell at a high price. The event was a crowded 'who's who' of producers, but the site was always clean, organized, and not lining you up with a future bout with lung disease.

My best memories of those conventions didn't involve the records I got, but the people I met. Godfather Don (a severely underrated hip-hop producer and artist with a strong niche following) and Herb McGruff (who rolled with Big L, Cam'Ron, and Ma$e, and later got a major label deal with Heavy D) had done a three song demo tape together that never came out. They were two cool and humble brothers who were just eager to promote their shit. Don gave me his last copy of the tape because I actually knew about his barely known *Hazardous* LP and asked him a million questions about it like a little fan boy. the demo was harder than finding a job and I still have it today. Apparently, neither Don nor McGruff have a copy,
or so I've heard.

6. Furniture Store on Warburton Avenue – Yonkers, NY (Defunct)

Yonkers could be the sixth borough of New York City. Directly north of the Northwest Bronx, it resembles The Bronx more than the Northwest Bronx. In the early '90s, the southwest quadrant of town near Getty Square offered a handful of seedy places to shop for second hand music. If you went out there on a digging mission, you'd want to dig and be out before it got dark.

Besides the fact that I found the entire Wild Pitch catalog on cassette (for $1 each) in the old Getty Square Woolworth's, there was a furniture shop right on the most dilapidated part of Warburton Ave., overlooking the Hudson River. I stumbled in dead in the middle of the Blizzard of 1996 and it was no warmer inside than it was outside. The inside was a dark, moldy, asbestos-laden nightmare, but they had some serious funk 45s in that joint. I found just about every Kool & the Gang 45 worth a listen in one giant box. There were also a bunch of obscure jazz fusion records, but of course they were beat to shit. I think I may have been the only collector who saw that place, because I wentback there in the spring and it had already been shut down. OSHA was probably notified when somebody croaked.

5. Short Lived Record Store, Name Unknown – New Rochelle, NY (Defunct)

I don't even remember the name of this joint. It opened in 1996 and it closed the same year. The owner was an old man who priced everything way too high and was a dick about people "manhandling" the records. That didn't matter much though, because I was cool with a DJ that was down with a local rap group, and his man was working in the store part-time. One day I was just browsing through records I couldn't afford when our DJ walks in. All he says is, "Just get whatever you want my nigga, it's on me." I knew the brother was in grime mode, but fuck asking questions. I took a stack of records worth about $500 and dumped 'em on the counter. The DJ took about seven crates of high-priced jazz and soul. All of a sudden, his friend pulls up in a big-ass *Sanford and Son* pick-up truck and money just starts loading. The whole time, the kid that's workin' there is like, "Y'all better hurry the fuck up, the owner is coming back!"

When I realized what was going down, I grabbed some more over-priced Blue Note joints I could sell downtown, hopped in the truck, and broke north. Those two dudes even gave me a ride home. I took all of the records I

177

got down to the city to sell and made a hell of a stack off them. It was enough to pay for my last few Drivers' Ed. classes, some new threads, and books for college in the fall. A week later, I went back to the spot and the shit was out of business. It serves that owner right; that's what he gets for trying to stick Manhattan tourist prices in New Ro.

4. Integrity 'n' Music - Weathersfield, CT

My pops lived in Connecticut for awhile; he put me on to this place when I went up there to visit. It was old, but super clean and extremely organized. Maybe Connecticut diggers pillaged this place, but I never heard anybody mention it. The owner didn't seem to like rap, so he priced it dirt cheap. Better for me, I got The 5th Platoon's "The Partyline" 12", The UBC's *2 All Serious Thinkers* LP, King Tee's *Tha Triflin' Album*, and Intelligent Hoodlum's "Black & Proud" 12", all for $1 total. All of those records (excluding the latter) are a bitch to find today, let alone cheap. They also had tons of dope kiddie records - I secured a mint copy of the *Roosevelt Franklin* album in there for $1 - and '70s jazz fusion. Most records cost $5 or less.

3. EX-DJ - New Rochelle, NY

One day in 1994, some brother (who was quite possibly smoking something) was outside Vee-Dubbs on Main St. with a crate of about 300 funk 45s. I'm not sure if he was on his way to get a fix, but he had joints worth turning down free health care for. Not just standards like James Brown, but Ricky Williams' "Discotheque Soul", The Pazant Bros.' "Chick-A-Boom", and a bunch of other limited press shit that costs a semester of state college today. He asked us for $100, but Vance and I talked him down to $50, if I remember correctly. We gave him $25 a piece and of course, I knew by label which 45s had beats on 'em. Again, I was a 17-year-old music nerd who knew more about which records had drums on them than how to get a girl to drop her drawers.

2. Out of the Past - Chicago, IL

If you decide to go here, don't go into the basement for an extreme length of time without a mask - you'll regret it. Don't ice grill anybody standing outside either - you'll regret it.

This may be my favorite record store in the world, but it's not for the squeamish, the impatient, the overly health conscious, or those who refuse to go to the hood. DJ Rude One put me on to this joint in the West Side of Chicago a few years back and when I went in there, I didn't know whether to turn my ass around for good or go get a hazmat suit and a sleeping bag and live there for a year. Before you even get inside, you'll spot the activity cameras lurking above your head on W. Madison Ave. Typically, a small posse of serious-looking brothers lurk out front grilling anybody that walks up in there. If you go during the winter, there may be some fur-clad old school pimps on the grind peddling pussy in the Chi-Town cold. You have the option of buying one of the $2 tall white tees in the store windows and when you get inside, you're bombarded with a 20 percent organized smorgasbord of cassettes, 8-track tapes, defunct toys, VHS tapes, stethoscopes, fly paper hung from the ceiling, James Brown 45 collages on the wall, random junk, and about a zillion albums. The first time I saw it, I had 20 minutes to look around before my flight home. I grabbed some super rare and regional gangsta rap tapes off the wall and a few local limited press funk 45s that were sitting on top of a discontinued board game with no board inside of it.

out of the past (2007)

I went back another time and took three steps into the infamous dungeon basement. The mold odor stopped me in my tracks, but I did see a bunch of sealed Syl Johnson LP's at the bottom of the staircase. Nonetheless, I valued my life too much to go all the way down. I've heard rumors that a dead bat (and a living one too), a UPS truck, and basically any album you want (if you're willing to put in the time and get into a brawl with your respiratory system) are down there.

If I ever knew I had a month left to live, I'd go down there with no protection and go out with a bang. I went with Rude and Large Professor once, and even Large (aka Digger Extraordinaire) took one look at the basement and said, "Man, fuck all that."

Prices vary, but I don't mind. The experience is as good as the selection and my trip to Chi-Town is incomplete without it. Every collector has to go there at least once or they haven't experienced what record hunting is all about. On that note, if I ever heard they organized that place or brought it up to code, I'd never go back. Don't no suckers dig there.

1. ALL Ears Records aka "The Diner" – New Brunswick, NJ (Defunct)

After a year of searching near and far for the first four Kool & the Gang albums to no avail, I resorted to the Yellow Pages. For whatever reason, the owner of All Ears had his New Jersey-based business listed as "Out Of Print Records" in the Manhattan phone book, so I gave him a buzz. Not only did he have every record I was looking for, but the prices weren't the standard Bleeker Bob's tourist trap ones. My pops spun me out there and the owner was sitting in a cluttered, raggedy-ass diner on French St. No browsing was allowed. You called, he went to "The Warehouse" to get the records and met you at the diner. The first Kool & the Gang album for $20 was a steal even back then, but now it goes for over $100. It's the most valuable piece of wax I own, but more so for the sentimental value. He threw in Kool's *Live at the Sex Machine*, *Live at PJ's*, and the first *Best Of ...* (with the gold mirror album cover) all for $80. I saved up for weeks for that trip and he held the records for me like a champ.

I have no idea when the man shut down shop, but I passed by the diner in 2007 and to my surprise, it was still standing. It was vacant of course, but it felt good to know that gentrification hadn't wiped out my own personal landmark...yet.

Digging doesn't play as prominent a role in my life as it once did, I'm man enough to admit it. It's not like I've traded in my dust mask for a mouse and shop online, but I've got more responsibility these days. Plus, with the few brick and mortar record stores left flailing to keep their lights on, there just isn't as much to dig through. Most of the true shit hole record stores that made digging a contact sport have closed. Nonetheless, these memories (among many others) will always define a huge chunk of who I am. Above all, they've embodied the thrill of attaining something when you get your hands dirty pursuing it. You gotta dig, ya dig?

25. I'M NOT AN EX-CON, I JUST LIKE TAPES

"Yo, where my killer tape at?" - Raekwon.

While sweatin' to the oldies at Planet Fitness (a notoriously bootleg gym chain) a few years back, some living room couch of a broad who was on the treadmill busted out laughing as I walked past her. I assumed I knew why, but I liked to think that there was really nothing wrong with using a Walkman in 2009.

"You just get out of prison or something?!" she shouted.

I didn't know what she meant at first, but when I got home later that night it hit me. Compact discs can also be cropped into nice little prison shanks, so cassettes were the safest medium for convicts to bump some tunes and thus became the lone music medium.

I got off dial-up internet in 2006. I purchased a cell phone that was more than $14 in 2010. Advancements in technology have always been given my boot upon their introduction to the masses, but I'm eventually backed into a corner and forced to get current. Look no further than my Twitter account, which I used to promote this book after making fun of the fruity little Tweety Bird and resisting the site like Wesley Snipes resisted Uncle Sam.

However, the jury is in when it comes to what I use to bang my tunes; I don't think I can ever make the complete switch to the iPod. I've been offered three of them for free over the past three years and refused them all. I eventually accepted a used iPod Shuffle from mom dukes. I tried it for a month before getting disgruntled because I couldn't find the songs on it. Even the look of the iPod doesn't suit me. When I think of them, I think of broads doing low-impact cardio on the elliptical machine at the gym. They're frail and dainty. You can't listen to Mob Style or Pretty Tone Capone on an iPod, it just doesn't make sense.

I can't ride with the thought of buying albums digitally and not getting physical liner notes, either. Album art and liner notes are just as a much part of the consumption of music as the music itself. There's nothing like buying a great album, then reading the liner notes and seeing Masta Ace playfully dis Mr. Cee for giving Big Daddy Kane the beat that was supposed to be his or who produced track #5. It's engaging to read Red Hot Lover Tone dissing all of the people he's supposed to be giving shout outs to. Reading the credits for Public Enemy's *Fear of a Black Planet*, I discovered new artists I had never heard of before by the categories they were placed in for the acknowledgments.

Seeing shout outs to people who weren't famous, but friends of the artist, was also a trip. These gentlemen had names like Big Ray Roll, Big Dog, and Psycho Pimp. You can't help but wonder what those three guys are contributing to society today. There's a good chance that they may run your child's day care center - that's a comforting thought.

I recently bought a CD re-issue of Kool & the Gang's *Live at PJ's* just for the bonus liner notes and never-seen-before photos. As fans, these are things we used to look forward to seeing when listening to music, but as for today's youth, I guess you can't miss what you've never been exposed to. Tell a 16-year-old kid about liner notes in 2011 and he'll think you're talking about boat instructions.

The closest thing we had to iTunes back in the day was the short-lived custom tape maker in the Sam Goody record store chain around 1990. Its proper name was The Personics System, and if you remember it, you're an OG because it lasted about a year. There was a book of selected songs from both popular artists and obscure up-and-comers; you ordered the songs you wanted to create a custom tape. I'd bullshit around the Galleria Mall in White Plains for an hour while they prepared my tape, then I'd come back to Sam Goody to pick up my funky new compilation. My first and only Personics System tape featured Freshco & Miz' "We Don't Play" and Uptown's "Dope on Plastic" and "It's My Turn." It's worth noting that those songs were never released on albums. Needless to say, The Personics System barely made it out of diapers before it was given the ax, presumably because most albums released back then were decent enough all the way through to warrant the $10 price tag. Albums were about peaks and valleys; you'd want to hear every nook and cranny of what an artist was about.

Tapes also hold a high level of significance in the development of hip-hop album structure. By 1990, they had taken over as the primary medium for bonus cuts like the 12" b-side did for vinyl. Albums like Stetsasonic's *Blood, Sweat & No Tears*, Nas' *It Was Written*, Digital Underground's *Sex Packets*, and Lord Finesse's *Return of the Funky Man* were all creatively marketed with cassette tape-only bonus cuts. The move gave you an incentive to hunt down the album in each format. There were even albums that only came out on cassette (the elusive Baritone Tip Love *Livin' Foul* album from 1991) or cassette

with a limited dose of wax, but no CD (MC Sergio's *Making A Killin'* and some of the Mob Style stuff).

I also miss buying tapes and seeing the order forms for merchandise from the groups and record labels inside of the fold out liner notes. The cassette inserts of the Luke Records (2 Live Crew, Poison Clan, etc.) releases were always my favorite. Luke was a visionary for racial harmony, as he had the junior high school cafeteria manager-looking, middle-aged brother standing side by side with the young, trampy white chick for his merchandising ads. Certain labels' (like Tommy Boy, for one) cassette tapes even had a distinct smell when you unfolded the j-card, a scent strong enough to hit you in the face without pressing your nose to the paper. These are defining moments of remembering an album that you just can't find in the milquetoast world of iTunes.

I ordered a "We Want Some Pussy" t-shirt before I lost my virginity, but I don't think the kid growing up now can experience the same rite of passage and that's foul. Raekwon had a purple tape, Masta Ace and I had gold tapes, and Illegal had a red tape, but I've never seen an MP3 with a color.

I'll play Devil's Advocate for the digital world when I speak from the view of the artist. Who really buys music in physical media form in 2011? Manufacturing music in any physical form and getting stuck with extra units could have you eating Ramen noodles for a year to survive. There are enough *To Love a Hooker* and *Boss Hog Barbarians* CDs in my basement to re-open a Crazy Eddie chain. Then again, my first two albums are near impossible to find and I get constant requests to re-press them. I put them on iTunes because its risk-free and saves me the hassle of getting stuck with overstock. It makes me seem like a hypocrite for plugging these releases on iTunes, because I don't even have an account there. It's a Catch 22 of things financially making sense and catering to the few fans like myself that still appreciate tapes, CDs, and LPs as part of the full music-buying experience.

Like everything else that was popular 20-25 years ago, there will be a small resurgence in tapes at some point. Folks may want to *Do the Right Thing* it all the way out and go get a ghetto blaster to be super-retro, but maybe tapes are too much of a hassle. Somebody will try to capture the aesthetic by making an iPod that sits inside of a ghetto blaster frame.

Oops, they already did.

Why didn't I see that coming when people began to go retro by mixing and matching trends from seven different eras into one outfit? I'm sure someone will have the audacity to bring back Africa medallions as well, just to let them pass as a fad again after six months. Only real OGs never stopped rolling with tapes and never will.

Rap is a generational phenomenon. A 14-year-old guitar player still digs on Hendrix. A 14-year-old saxophonist still digs on Coltrane. A 14-year-old rapper wouldn't know Kool G. Rap if G. Rap put out a cigar on his forehead. If you're 18 years old, you'll say Nicki Minaj won her rap war with Lil' Kim. If you're 28 years old, you'll say Kim was the victor. If you're 42 years old, you'll say MC Lyte would've barbecued both of those bitches or you won't give a shit at all because your kid's tuition is due. Rap folks will eight times out of ten relate to the era they came up in above all, and while the phasing out of cassette tapes was a natural progression for some, the old habits I acquired just die way too hard.

In summation, until Disco Rick & The Dogs' entire catalog is available on iTunes with 20 unreleased bonus cuts, I'll keep being mistaken for an ex-convict. Although I won't try to sell you a rickety bridge via a VHS tapes vs. DVDs argument, I didn't see O-Dog passing around a DVD of the liquor store robbery in *Menace II Society*. Just a thought.

26. FUNKY GRANNY

Senior citizens.

They drive you 730 when they hold up lines for days on end in the supermarket. Or, if for some reason they're still allowed on the road (that has to be outlawed), they'll drive 27 MPH in the left lane of a 65 MPH zone and spoil your day. Well, what about living with one for well over a decade?

Since Arnold Sr. passed away in '97, I've been living with and looking after my grandmother. If I were to compare our relationship to anything in popular culture, it would be that of Fred and Lamont Sanford's on the TV show *Sanford and Son.* In just about every episode, Fred's hypochondriac complaints, far-fetched schemes to make or save money, and dislike for everyone not named Fred got him and Lamont into a pit of shit. Lamont often threatened to move out on Fred to live the bachelor-esque lifestyle of his peers, but for all of the aggravation, he always stuck around and just dealt with the cantankerous old man.

Day-to-day affairs for my grandmother (who was donned with the nickname "Evil E" long before I roamed the Earth) and I aren't much different (or any less deserving of a reality show pilot) than those of Fred and Lamont. I woke up to daily requests to go to the store to get reduced price Glucerna and All-Bran while my peers lived their post-college party animal lives in NYC's hippest enclaves. People would crack jokes about my situation over the years, but it's a matter of culture and customs. Where I come from, you don't put Grandma in a nursing home; you give her a room in your house until she can no longer do for herself. At 87 years of age, Evil E is still on her feet and vicious, albeit a step slower and growing more thoroughly insane each day.

My part-time job throughout my 20s was doing damage control for Evil E's Fred-like body of work. There was the time she pulled out a book of 17 expired coupons in the supermarket and demanded the coupons be accepted, before calling the cashier "ignorant" and hurling racial epithets at nobody in particular. Her long-running penchant for putting her foot a mile deep in somebody's ass has never lost steam with age. In fact, her arthritis only intensified her ability to thrash, because now she uses that cane for everything except walking and still keeps a taped up Louisville Slugger bat by her bedroom door in case "somebody comes up in here."

However, her favorite target is the one she can hit at close range, and that would be me. If I'm not getting lambasted because Wal-Mart didn't have something that she sent me for, I'm getting sent to six different stores in two different counties for seven different items to save $1.17. That's not as bad as when I took her to the stores so she could shop for "a few items" herself, though. After two hours of cussing out store managers and running over fellow shoppers with an overloaded cart, a reminder from me that she was only supposed to get "a few items" was answered with a "shut up."

She's also mastered the art of the buzz kill. Evil E usually waits until I'm eating to explain aloud how bran muffins help her get "a nice smooth bowel movement" or until I go to her part of the house for something to start farting and saying, "ooooh, listen to the gas" with the same level of satisfaction as a convict getting his first free world nut. When she gets extra perturbed, she may come after me without her false teeth in her mouth and it's comparable to being chased by a black female Popeye on a rampage or Ms. Pac-Man after she ate an energy pellet.

She's recently come down with a bad bout of carpal-tunnel syndrome. It's bothersome to watch her suffer, but sometimes I wonder if she'd be in that medical predicament had she not popped me upside my head for 33 years.

My grandmother is nosy and loves to ask questions. When I respond, she always cuts me off mid-sentence.

"Huh? I can't understand what you're saying."

I think she does it just to fuck with my head, because if I fail to answer in less than ten seconds, she responds to my response. She heard me the first time; she just does the shit habitually. When I call her on it, she just changes the subject.

Old folks are always cold, making them nearly impossible to live with in the winter. I wake up in pools of sweat because she insists on keeping the thermostat on 82 degrees. She'll cook something and leave our already metal-barred windows completely shut, so "nobody can come up in here." Meanwhile, she's still freezing and I'm subject to be dead from heat exhaustion.

Of course there was the time she thought she was allergic to Niacin (a B vitamin that appears in everything) and ordered me to throw out all things in the house that contained it. She was later told by her doctor that trace amounts wouldn't hurt her. Guess who had to go out the next day to replace everything

190

that was just thrown out? At least she didn't drop a stankin' turd in my car like she did my in father's rental. Pops had a jolly ole time getting the stench out of that Ford Focus before returning it to Budget Rent-A-Car. Her logic?

"When I gotta go, I gotta go," she said without a smidgen of guilt. "The Lord said it's time to move my bowels, so I moved them."

She's even more of a trip when it comes to my personal life, and has Fred Sanford's knack for cock-blocking as well.

"I don't want no hanky panky down there."

That's usually how she tried to stop me from bringing bimbos home to smash in my 20s. She never stopped me, though.

"You think you're slick bringin' them girls up in here."

The average grown-ass man would be embarrassed, but not I. She still acts like I have a curfew, but she doesn't expect me to obey her. It's a grandmotherly quality that's the same now as it was when I was 12. It will undoubtedly remain that way if she lives to see me reach 74.

For all our daily friction, she's also taught me things about life that I never learned during my years on the NYC nightlife scene or my decade and change in the music business. Let's not forget, giving me money to record my first demo and putting up with my knucklehead shit for so many years are no miniature feats. However, the cake-taker is her never-ending benevolence when it comes to providing family and friends with a roof overhead. The same house that she and Arnold Sr. bought in 1964 has always been presented as "home" to me, regardless of where else I laid my 'fro to the pillow. Grandparents and parents typically have the same level of duty and importance in the black family structure, with the latter sometimes taking on an even lesser parental role than the former.

Seniors are OGs in the game. If they didn't know what life was all about, they wouldn't have lived so long. The shit my grandmother has endured over the last 87 years would break today's woman. Arnold Sr. didn't live to see our 14 year (and counting) system in action, but he'd be happy to know his wife of 50 years is in decent hands by way of his sons and grandson, despite my occasional tendency to be a lazy piece of shit around the house.

For those of you with living grandparents, call 'em up today and give 'em some OG love. Love? Yeah, even curmudgeons and villains have the capacity to do that...just not very often.

Thank you, Evil E - The Matriarch of our family.

BONUS BEATS

J-ZONE'S DISCOGRAPHY

Music for Tu Madre (1999) - Old Maid Entertainment; *A Bottle of Whup Ass* (2000) - Old Maid Entertainment; *Pimps Don't Pay Taxes* (2001) - Old Maid Entertainment; *$ick of Bein' Rich* (2003) - Old Maid Entertainment / Fat Beats Records; *A Job Ain't Nuthin but Work* (2004) - Old Maid Entertainment / Fat Beats Records; *Gimme Dat Beat Fool: The J-Zone Remix Project* (2005) - Zone Records; *Every Hog Has Its Day* (w/ Celph Titled as Boss Hog Barbarians) (2006) - Hog Cabin / Mt. Kill-A-Ho Ent.; *Experienced!* (2006) - Bootleg; *To Love a Hooker: The Motion Picture Soundtrack* (2006) - Old Maid Entertainment; J-Zone Presents… *Chief Chinchilla: Live at the Liqua Sto* (2008) - Old Maid Entertainment

J-ZONE'S (SELECTED) OUTSIDE PRODUCTION CREDITS

Preacher Earl & The Ministry: "Fool I Got Your Back" (1995)
Cage: "In Stoney Lodge" (2002)
Biz Markie: "Chinese Food" (2003)
Tame One: "Heat", "Tame As It Ever Was" & "Slick Talkin" (2003)
RA The Rugged Man: "Brawl" (2003)
Prince Po: "It's Goin' Down" & "Meet Me At The Bar" (2003)
MF Grimm (aka GM Grimm): "Taken" & "Dancing" (2003)
Akinyele: "Ak-Nel" & "In The Zone" (2004)
Casual: "Say That Then" & "Hieroller" (2005)
Sadat X: "X Is A Machine" (2006)
Del the Funkee Homosapien: "Funkyhomosapien" (2008)
Lonely Island: "Santana DVX" (Featuring E-40) (2009)
Mr. Lif: "Gun Fight" (2009)
Cunninlinguists: "Cocaine" (2010)

J-ZONE'S (SELECTED) PUBLISHED WORKS

"5 Things That Killed Hip-Hop"; *Common Culture (Sixth Edition)*; Prentice Hall, 2009
"Ign'ant (Monthly Column)"; *Hip-Hop Connection (HHC)* Magazine (UK); 2001-2004

"Foreword"; *Gangster Rap Coloring Book*; Last Gasp, 2004
"Selected articles"; *SLAM Magazine*, 2007-2009

J-zone's social Network crap

Official Website: www.govillaingo.com
Twitter: www.twitter.com/jzonedonttweet
Blog: www.egotripland.com/author/j-zone
Facebook: www.facebook.com/jzone101

J-Zone Fan Club
Old Maid Entertainment
P.O. Box 110524
Cambria Heights, NY 11411

J-zone's shouts

Peace to those who took the time to help me bring this book to fruition: James Blackwell, Alexander Richter, Jeff Mao, Sam Slaughter, Nick Diunte, Keecha Patrick, John Everette, Moe Choi, Lilly Simon, Kevin Young, David "Rekstizzy" Lee and Ed Wong. Thanks y'all. IHOP is on me, but stay on the cheap side of the menu.

To Dad for lifelong creative encouragement, to Mom for being there, to Grandma and the rest of my family for their support. Shouts to Cory Carter, Tone Tran, Kevin Severe, Alex Zephyr, Bevan Jee, Peter Klein, Ivan Yizar, Brian Charles, Breeze Brewin, Rick Feltes, Al-Shid, Celph Titled. Shouts to The HHC Crew, Dante Ross, The ego trip crew, Aye Jay, Hip-Hop DX, the SLAM Magazine crew, Maurice Wingate, and everyone else who has given me a platform as a writer. Shouts to all who support me in any shape or form.

All proceeds from this book will go to a real cause - putting Mitch "Blood" Green on a postage stamp.

ABOUT THE AUTHOR

J-ZONE is a connoisseur of humbling reality checks, lesser-known rap albums from the early '90s, self-deprecation, and full-fledged lampoonery. His primary hobby is assailing our daily acts of bullshit. Throughout his decade and change in the music business, he's worked with the likes of Gnarls Barkley, The Lonely Island, Biz Markie, E-40, and Prince Paul, to name a few. As a writer, his work has been published in the Common Culture pop culture textbook series, SLAM Magazine, The Source, and London's Hip-Hop Connection (HHC), among others. He's a regular contributor for ego trip NYC and moonlights as a high school sports reporter in the New York Metropolitan area. J-Zone has also taught music classes in the SUNY (State University of New York) system. He's an insubordinate curmudgeon and a New York native who will invoice you if you send him emoticon and acronym-laden text messages. He lives in Queens, New York with his beloved grandmother, "Evil E".